Natural Learning

Copyright © Jane Evans 2022

First Published 2022 by Flutterby Books

All rights reserved.

No part of this book may be reproduced or transmitted in any form or by any means, electronic or mechanical, including photocopying, recording or by any information storage and retrieval system, without prior permission in writing from the publisher.

A catalogue record for this book is available from the National Library of New Zealand.

Soft cover ISBN 978-0-473-61630-4
Soft cover POD ISBN 978-0-473-61631-1
Epub ISBN 978-0-473-61632-8

Cover art by Duncan Hill

This book has been printed using sustainably managed stock.

Design & layout www.yourbooks.co.nz

Printed in New Zealand by www.yourbooks.co.nz

Natural Learning
THE UNSCHOOLING LIFE

Jane Evans

Flutterby

To my mother Diana, a natural learner at heart,
for her relaxed and trusting approach as a parent

For the things we have to learn before we can do them, we learn by doing them.
— *Aristotle*

CONTENTS

Acknowledgements iii
Preface v
Introduction... vii
What is natural learning? 1
The benefits of natural learning 12
Being the parent of a natural learner 31
Philosophy, values and family culture 49
Creating a learning environment 64
Comparisons and unhelpful questions 84
Reading, writing and maths 93
Science in play 112
Learning is everywhere and in everything 117
Measuring progress 130
Setting limits with technology 139
Navigating the teenage years 145
Gaining formal qualifications 158
Feeling the joy 164
Beyond the imagination years 171
A wish for the joyful life 185
Further reading 186

ACKNOWLEDGEMENTS

My thanks to Linda Cassells for her editing expertise, support and encouragement. Working with her felt like a crash course in writing.

Special acknowledgment to my creative cousin, Vicki Gray, at Blumango Creative for her generous and enthusiastic design input in producing the Flutterby Publishing logo.

So much gratitude to great friend, artist and fellow natural learner, Duncan Hill for his creative energy and care in designing the original cover.

Ngā mihi nui to Playcentre in Aotearoa New Zealand, which was our whānau (family) for years and years. I learned so much and was inspired by everyone I met and worked with while we raised our young children together.

Thank you to those in Hearthland Educators, past and present, as well as to our nationwide community of natural learners. I am forever grateful for the networks of support I have had and continue to have. Their stories also feature in this book, woven into the text in innumerable ways. Special thanks to Toni Bragg, Madz BatachEl and Suzanne Chelius for permission to use their stories here and to Krista Fullerton and Suzanne Chelius for their reading of the manuscript in its early stages.

Deep recognition and respect to my wonderful older kids, Dane and Kim, for their loving support of me as a young parent. I wish I could have shared natural learning with both of them as well. I am so proud of all they now are and their commitment to their own parenting journeys.

My loving gratitude to the three protagonists in this story: Hannah, Ollie and Charlie for choosing me. What a wild and wonderful ride we have had. Thank you for the shared love, the memories, the laughs and adventures. There would be no book without them.

My thanks and appreciation to Wayne. This book would never have happened without his support over many years, of his working and enabling the things I wanted to do, the time I devoted to the children, and the life we led. I am forever grateful to be sharing five amazing children with him.

My thanks to the following for permission to quote copyrighted material: Denise Gaskins for her quote in Chapter 7, page [107]70+ Things To Do with a Hundred Chart: Number, Shape, and Logic Activities from Preschool to Middle School, Tabletop Academy Press, 2018 www.denisegaskins.com ; The Association Montessori Internationale for the quote in Chapter 5, page [82] from Citizen of the World, Montessori-Pierson Publishing Company, 2019,page 31, and in Chapter 4, page [58] from Maria Montessori Speaks to Parents, Montessori-Pierson Publishing Company, 2019 page 18.

PREFACE

After being inspired by a book of natural learning stories, I too wish to share ours. I know I am not alone in feeling heartened when hearing other people's stories and hope this book gives even one family the confidence to raise their children with natural learning at the heart. I have been lucky enough to experience first-hand a commitment to respectful and child-centred parenting from many other parents. Their desire and confidence to break away from the norm and live with integrity is to be applauded and I want to lend my support to anyone who takes this path.

When the kids were growing up I enjoyed keeping a blog that documented our lives of natural learning, recording stories and experiences on our journey. This formed the basis for my notes for this book. Some stories have become part of our family's folklore and others are cemented in my memory forever because of their sheer beauty. I have also spent many hours answering questions and hearing concerns from parents of young children who are homeschooling in some way and who know they want to embrace natural learning. From this interaction I realised how much fear and anxiety many people harbour – in many cases a hangover from one parent's own school days. I have incorporated the lessons I have learned from our personal experiences around the most common concerns that parents raised. I also understand that knowing someone who is a few years ahead of you on a similar parenting journey can offer much value and comfort.

Many different possible paths may have led you to this book. Perhaps you are a parent who wants more time with your child. You can see how the way they play is fundamental to their development, and you may be considering natural learning. Perhaps your children are already doing 'school at home', but you feel there is more to life than formal book learning. Or maybe you miss your rapidly growing children and now they are at school you find you have no time to go on adventures or curl up together and read for hours. Whatever stage of the parenting journey you are at, it is never too late or too early, to shake things up, question the status quo and follow your heart.

Sometimes in life you need a gentle nudge, and sometimes you just need to hear the right story.

INTRODUCTION

I was a teacher in a state primary school, a positive, high-energy, empathetic and child-centred teacher. I loved teaching. For me it was all about people, mostly young 11-13-year-old people. Even before I had my own children, I understood at some level the importance of being child-centred when teaching and how vital it is for children to be empowered. I recognised how useless it was to try to teach anyone who is not interested in learning.

At that time, I was frustrated with the education system – the huge workload, the testing, the administration and the expectation that I was to plan, deliver and assess nine subjects to over 30 young people. Much of my spare time was spent creating an inspiring learning environment and planning engaging, hands-on educational opportunities for students. Seeing their diverse needs made me want to create an individual programme for each of them, which was impossible within a school setting.

During my years as a primary school teacher, I

also became aware of children whom I felt did not have quality time with their parents. I worked in a predominantly white, reasonably wealthy middle-class area where the majority of children had spent their pre-school lives in a daycare, with their working parents commuting an hour to the city for work. These children could have had anything that money could buy. What these students taught me, and what I instinctively learned through spending so much time with them, was that they needed to have their parents spend time with them, as they did when they were babies and toddlers. The longer I taught the clearer it became. After banging my head against a brick wall day after day, I remember one day saying to myself, 'I am going to leave, have my own children and be there to give them my time.'

While teaching, I came to understand deeply how each person has their own passions, skills, personalities, limits, triggers and needs. I wanted to be able to treat each person as an individual so they could flourish and grow. I saw no way to facilitate this in the system I was in, try as I might. I saw the light go out in the eyes of those whom I stood over, using my power as an adult to insist on their finishing pointless work. I also saw the spark, the energy and the passion to learn in the eyes of those that were on fire with a project or an idea of their own devising, when they were lit up with excitement. I remember one student in particular who struggled academically but who was desperate for a class pet. He became motivated to fundraise, while using a wide range of skills. I saw the value in this and let him spend school time pursuing it, with the whole class benefitting from his endeavours of introducing different class pets, amazing cages and plentiful food supplies. It was a huge learning opportunity for this student; I loved seeing a child so motivated and engaged and continued to nurture this sort of learning as much as possible. Child-led learning brings with it great joy. It made a lot of sense to me and is still one of the highlights of my teaching.

When I left full-time teaching, I moved into parenting with a ready-made family. I was lucky to inherit two step-children and then go on to give birth to three more children, who are the ones in our family who have experienced the natural learning lifestyle. When the youngest was born we set off in a house bus to travel for 18 months around Aotearoa New Zealand. Before this trip was over the oldest child had turned six, so I applied to homeschool her. This was our first introduction to homeschooling. It made no difference to our lives at all, she just carried on doing what she did, mostly reading, and we continued travelling. We were already embracing natural learning but didn't know it.

A few months after our trip had ended, we bought a property and settled down. I was feeling overwhelmed with a new house, a big garden and three young children, so the older two, aged five and seven, went to school. I was attending Playcentre with the youngest and felt it was too much to juggle all three children at home. The older children had already had some homeschooling experience and often asked to be taken out of school. This led to me feeling guilty much of the time, and I felt sad that school wasn't meeting their needs. I also missed them when they were at school.

With them being away all day, we had little quality

time as a family. I wondered how we would get to do all the things I had imagined and planned. Both children were exhausted by the weekend and didn't want to socialise. They just wanted to play, usually quietly, with just the three of them together or alone. It took me two years before I took the plunge and let them leave school. The older children are now philosophical about that early time at school, insisting it has made them appreciate the life that followed even more.

I am a passionate teacher and I know there are many wonderful teachers in the world. I do not wish to undermine the positive work that so many teachers are doing under sometimes challenging conditions. They make a difference to so many lives. I am also grateful to the many teachers who understand the benefits of child-led learning and are working to create a new way to learn in our schools.

So with four-year-old Charlie, seven-year-old Ollie and nine-year-old Hannah we started officially homeschooling. I felt relaxed about having to do anything too structured, and at the beginning of the school year we sat down and played 'school at home'. This meant desks, books, timetables and projects, which for years afterwards Charlie often asked if we could 'play' again.

Three weeks into this new regime I read the book Free Range Learning: How Homeschooling Changes Everything by Laura Grace Weldon. This is an English book documenting stories of children who had left the school system and were now living a relaxed life often referred to as 'natural learning' or 'unschooling'. The parents had written about the experiences their children had had at school which caused unhappiness, loss of confidence and stress. I read about children going backwards academically and being bullied or being bored. I read about natural learning and how these children now lived and learned without a curriculum, testing or timetable, and how they had flourished.

I read solidly through the night and by 3.00am I had finished the book. I was buzzing with excitement and my heart was full of knowing that this was the way for our family. I was longing to tell someone, to shout it out to the world that we had a new plan and a new life to explore. It was my epiphany, and I could barely contain my relief, my elation and my gratitude. I told the children the next day that we were throwing out the workbooks they had been writing in and never doing that again. The older two looked at me as if to say, 'Oh, finally you figured that out.'

It was a big jump to make. There was no safety net so it was not a decision to be made lightly. I was trusting that although I did not know exactly how this natural learning path looked and how it would pan out, I knew it had to begin with us spending more time together and with happy children. And yet the decision was as easy as falling over. I followed my heart and as my children were part of me, they came along for the ride. We moved into a new life together, but in many ways, I felt as though we were getting our old life back.

While I had an instant moment of recognition, knowing this was the right path for us, it didn't mean it was plain sailing. Here was this new and radical way of educating your children, one that sat well within me, and I knew was perfect for us, yet there was no blueprint to follow. After I finished reading the book I didn't know instantly how to facilitate natural learning with my children. When I finished it, I realised I was at the start of a journey of discovery. The 'how' was not yet written for us, but the 'what' and 'why' were clearly laid out like a challenge that I accepted without hesitation.

As we embraced the natural learning life, I had moments of uncertainty, doubts and at times even panic. On Monday mornings I knew that 400 children down the road were doing maths, while my kids were doing what? Nothing? Cuddling their new baby guinea pigs? The book I had read was an inspiration to me, but it told other people's stories. We now had to create our own stories and walk our own path. It was refreshing, but at times terrifying too.

For the first few months I kept a diary. I wrote titbits throughout the day. 'Kids very happy swimming. Talked about the history of the area. Asking questions about the moon/dog training/camouflage. Played Monopoly. Making a book. Picking pears. Washing the car. Reading all day. Playing Lego for five hours. Making pizza. Reading Harry Potter.' I could see that learning was taking place, yet it took time for me to let go completely. I was still comparing their learning with what I knew happened in a typical classroom.

Whenever I had doubts, when it seemed as though the kids had 'done nothing', I would read my notes which would calm and reassure me. After four months I arrived at a place where I felt confident in myself and in the natural learning approach. I trusted the children and their individual journeys, which meant their decision-making about how they spent their days. I could see that their everyday play, their games and creativity were packed full of learning. I understood how each of them took the time they needed to complete a project and how even a simple conversation was rich in learning. We could now relax and get on with living our chosen life of great freedom.

The children became 'passion chasers', following their own hearts and own interests, no matter how fleeting or small. They have grown and learned while developing into independent young people. At the same time, they taught me much about the process of natural learning and what is important in life. I am still constantly challenged by them – they are the greatest teachers around. They tell me what they need, what I should and shouldn't be doing, and how to go about it. During the years of natural learning, each child brought their own perspective, knowledge and personality to the table to share, and if you cared to look, learning was happening all the time. It came from their play, it came from friends, from books and from observation of the world around them. I certainly answered a huge number of their questions, while at other times they would discover the answers themselves, talking to a sibling or a visiting family member. By giving them the space to pursue their own interests, I too was able to pursue mine, which in turn was good role-modelling for them, and so the cycle continued over the years.

As you will also see as you read this book, they have also turned out okay. They have achieved 'success', academic and otherwise, which is measurable in the mainstream. This is helpful to illustrate how natural learning can eventually look for those starting out. Importantly, each child has a strong sense of self. They are sure of who they are, of what they enjoy and how they learn. They get on well with people of all ages and from all walks of life and are confident in new situations. A big bonus are the close relationships we now share as a family after spending those early, formative years together. Quality time with an interested adult seems to be exactly what children need in order to thrive. Looking back now, it seems like our life was a dream. It still is a wonderful life, full of freedom, fun and learning.

Chapter 1

WHAT IS NATURAL LEARNING?

Coming up with a definition of natural learning is difficult. How do you define what we do? Many group discussions and conversations in various forums have tried over the years to find a label for the way we raise and educate our children, but never with a satisfactory outcome for everyone. This natural way of raising children, essentially allowing them to educate themselves, mostly defies definition. There are times when a definition can be handy. Some terms you may come across are: natural learning, lifelong learning, passion chasing, world schooling, no-school, or unschooling. I prefer to use the term 'natural learning' as an apt description of the way our children have lived and learned, and for ease will use it throughout the book.

The term 'unschooling' is commonly used, and is interchangeable with natural learning. It was coined in the 1970s by John Holt, an American teacher and author of over a dozen books, mostly on education. He worked in private schools and believed that fear of failure, fear of appearing stupid and fear of criticism from both children and adults was what drove the education system. The fear that many students feel in school inhibits learning in his view and leads to the creation of what he called the 'charade of learning' in schools. This takes the form of testing, ticking boxes, filling in reports and grading students. He was an advocate of child-led education and is often referred to as the 'father of unschooling'. John Holt has explained, described, promoted and experimented with unschooling extensively, and for those readers wanting to know more, some of his works are listed in the Further Reading section at the end of the book.

As a definition of a whole educational philosophy, 'unschooling' is, however, a misnomer in my view. It is a strange name to give such a wild and free lifestyle. It tells you nothing of what is happening, only what is not, yet the term 'unschooling' has gained traction and is a handy label when searching online for resources and support.

What constitutes educating your children at home varies greatly from family to family. The stereotypical image is of a mini school at home, where children work on their computers or on their books at the kitchen table from 9.00am through to 3.00pm, five days a week. A natural learner who is following their own desires may well enact this exact scenario, even for a short time. Natural learning may mean a child takes classes and courses in various ways when it suits them. They may enrol in online forums or attend a workshop with adult participants. A child may even go to school for a time. Natural learners often try out school to see how it differs from their life and whether it has anything to offer them.

The difference for natural learners is that when school no longer serves them or meets their needs they are free to change what they do and know they are supported in this. A parent of a natural learner will assist their child to go to school if they wish, as much as they will also allow them to leave when they need to.

Natural learning can be a difficult concept to get to grips with. It can be mind-blowing to imagine a whole childhood passing without any testing, formal lessons and class structure. Trying to understand how it works may require some re-learning from you, the parent, to be able to relax and trust your children on their own learning paths. If you were educated in the school system or if you have never encountered any natural learners, you may feel uncomfortable letting your children choose to do what they want. If you are surrounded by fear-mongering nay-sayers, within your broader family or through your circle of friends, then you will have to find the inner strength to stand up and defend your right to raise your offspring out of school in this way.

Natural learning is just that – learning about the world naturally. It is simply letting your child do what they want, when they want, for as long as they want, and supporting them in that, all within the context of your family life. It is based on the idea that a person learns best when they are interested, intrinsically motivated and see the relevance of what they are doing. Natural learning is a journey of ups and downs. It ebbs and flows with your child and their changing interests while fitting in alongside your own life.

No fancy equipment is needed and no special training is required to become a natural learning family. As a parent, you raise your child to the best of your ability, within your culture, your belief system, your values and lifestyle. A child's journey of discovery will reflect all this while also being influenced by every book you read to them, every person that speaks to them, every song they hear and every item that they touch. As children crawl, climb, eat, ask questions, create, listen and use all their senses to understand their surroundings, learning arrives through the filter of your home, your community and the life you share with them.

Natural learning is a multi-directional process. It flows from parent to child, from child to child and from child to parent. Extended family, the community and even random strangers all contribute to everyday learning experiences. It is far removed from the model of an adult 'teaching' or dictating to a child. As a parent of natural learners, you will also gain much from living alongside your children, even if your learning outcomes are different. No doubt you will learn from the interesting array of topics that flow into your home via your children, but perhaps too you may learn about patience, trust, listening and slowing down.

An easy way to illustrate how natural learning works is to look at a baby's development. How and why does a baby learn to walk? Walking is a complex process consisting of many different physical and mental components that need great coordination. A baby wants to walk because they are surrounded by walkers. They see what happens in the world and they want to be part of it. A baby is only making sense of what they see and copying that. This is how we are all programmed to learn.

WHAT IS NATURAL LEARNING?

Do you remember when your baby started to walk? Did you trust and expect that they would walk when they were ready? Even if your child started walking at a different age to what the accepted measurement of 'normal' was, were you patient, positive, calm and supportive? Yes, of course you were. No doubt you gave them plenty of time and space to practise, staggering between two of you sitting on the lounge floor. You would have cheered them on and helped them by walking at their pace, holding their tiny hand for hours on end. You didn't berate them when they fell over a hundred times, you didn't test them against their peers. You quietly moved breakables higher up and enjoyed witnessing the miracle of natural learning as they edged their way around furniture. You followed their lead and trusted them, and your brilliant baby walked when they were ready.

How does a baby learn to speak? Do you really think that anything else they do in life will be harder than speaking for you to model or for them to learn? If you have parented a young child, then you have been their first teacher and their inspiration, whether you like it or not. The spectrum of when and how young children learn to speak is wide and varied. Maybe your baby learned to speak from non-stop babbling that turned into clear speech at two, three or four years of age. Or perhaps they were silent until they uttered a full sentence when they were ready. Parents instinctively understand that a baby needs to be surrounded by speech to learn the skill. We naturally repeat phrases and words and encourage them to say our names or those of common objects.

For a young child life is a process of constant illumination while they make sense of the world around them. Raising a child is like living in an experiment that clearly shows you, the parent, an outcome in the form of concrete results. You see that by engaging in conversation from birth, reading books to babies and explaining what you can see around you shapes their language. From your early 'this is a blue hat' or 'look at the big dog' their first words will reflect their experience of the world. I have been interested in the growing number of young children starting to speak at the age of two or three with an American accent acquired from television. Whatever your child is listening to, they will absorb and repeat, much like a parrot.

Natural learning is an instinctive continuation from walking and talking. Whatever else a child will learn follows on from these two building blocks – whether it is riding a bike, learning to cook, or advanced physics. When they are interested and self-motivated, a child's learning will unfold with your support. If you as a parent have a walking, talking, active, interested young child, then you are ahead of the game and already giving them the best thing in the world, the one thing they need and crave: YOU – your time, love, smiles, hugs, care, laughter and full, genuine attention.

WHAT DOES NATURAL LEARNING LOOK LIKE?

Living a life of freedom each day can be anything you desire and everything you ever imagined. It is an integral part of your life, not something that is sectioned off for a specific time of the day or restricted to five days a week. Natural learning is simply parenting; it is full time and often intense. The unknown and the potential of each day is refreshing, no matter how much rhythm your lives may have. The unexpected, often driven by a child's curiosity, keeps you grounded, possibly well entertained and hopefully mentally stimulated enough to fully enjoy the time you spend together.

Sometimes a question or a comment from someone is enough to spawn a new project for your child. Their interest may have been sparked by something from a book, and it may be fleeting or long lasting. Natural learning may not look like any learning you have ever experienced before, but sometimes all you have to go on is trusting that glimmer in your child's eyes, their persistence with a project or their flow of questions. Natural learning can be anything from a brief conversation to a years-long, evolving, messy, hands-on manifestation of creativity or discovery – and everything in between.

There will be days when you feel like the world's best parent, days that flow easily when everyone is happily occupied playing and creating. The rhythm and flow of your days and weeks will be determined by many factors: where you live, your community, your personalities and the needs of each member of your family.

NO TYPICAL DAY
A happy day for me was one where I could garden, bake and get household chores done while supporting the kids who were engaged in their own play. If I could manage to answer most of their questions and produce the resources they needed, while meeting some of my own needs, however small, with a family walk to the river, this for us was always the blissful day of natural learning,

living and parenting. Equally, a full day out in nature with our natural learning group, perhaps running in the forest or on the beach at Wild Child, a Forest School, playing games, lighting fires and building huts was always a perfect day too. A town day of various shopping jobs, swimming lessons, ballet lessons and time at the library meant we lived out of the car all day and returned home tired but satisfied.

As for any parent, doubts may bubble up about your ability to do this job. You may feel overwhelmed or like a failure. If your children are with you all day, you may wonder what you are doing with your own life, or think how selfish you are ruining your children's chances at a regular education. There will be days when no one gets dressed, when you're too tired to get anything done and you eat toast all day. There will also be days when it seems you don't know the answers to anything they ask, and you still worry that they may never know what a square root is. But these are also regular days in the life of any parent. Feelings and insecurities can be amplified when parenting is a full-time job.

SCHEDULES

As the kids grew, so did our weekly commitments which saw us tied into the school terms as much as anybody else. Drama, dance, martial arts, music lessons and Scouts all created the rhythm of our week, which meant that mornings were slow and easy and late afternoons were often spent in the car and eating dinner on the run, or later, like many

> families. While some natural learners resist these organised, extracurricular activities, others see it as an opportunity to embrace them and manage to fit in plenty of afternoon and evening classes. I have friends with five children who all take dance classes. Their schedule is mind boggling and their evenings are spent based at the dance studio, as each child is in several classes, with additional trips across town to fit in music lessons. Being natural learners gives the children the time and chance to embrace these passions.

There may be no typical day or a string of days the same. The freedom of natural learning is in the power you have to co-create and shape your days however you and your children desire throughout the years of their childhood.

HOW DOES IT FEEL?

People are generally interested in how natural learning works in practice. Appearances can be deceiving. Feelings are what guide me in everyday life, from the tiniest niggles to making life-changing decisions. Your feelings will be picked up by your children and may be responsible for creating the atmosphere in your home. This is your life too, so it is vital that you enjoy the ride. If you feel happy and content while spending time with your children and can relax while they play, then you provide a solid foundation for their development. If you are the sort of parent who can let your child get on with their day without you experiencing undue anxiety, then you will probably feel positively towards how natural learning will work for you all.

Checking in with yourself and how you feel is good practice and one that is often ignored while parenting. I suggest it is given priority and addressed as a starting point. Although parenting is not quite as simplistic as 'happy parents, happy kids', in many respects this scenario rings true. We all have the good and bad moments in between the mundane routines. When your children are an active part of this everyday flow, then it becomes necessary to include them in the reality of what is happening, not airbrush life with a magic wand of positivity. A real-life approach will serve to enrich all your lives and help you to be true to yourself.

A family is a dynamic group, where timing can make all the difference. Sometimes simply trusting that things will change in the future and being open to that possibility is a good start. It is good to remember 'this too shall pass'. Everything moves on and changes, whether you perceive it in a positive or negative light. Everything is transitory, so enjoying what is here now makes sound sense. Being in the present is a basic spiritual practice that your children will benefit from and possibly pick up on.

HOW IT FEELS

Natural learning and being with my children most of the time as they grew and changed has been a magical mix of intensity and ease, of freedom and connection. A relaxed lifestyle offers simplicity and a depth of experience that can only evolve through sharing so much of your lives together. The feeling of being with my children all day, each day, is one that for me was wholly fulfilling.

I enjoyed feeling secure and safe with no concerns about their wellbeing, emotional or otherwise. This meant I was most happy and relaxed when we were together; I was a better parent, and the ripple effects were positive.

Full-time parenting and natural learning is a mix of all the things that you feel and all that your children are feeling too. It is 'doing' life in all its glory but with inquisitive, creative, loving little people there alongside you every step of the way.

Chapter 2

THE BENEFITS OF NATURAL LEARNING

In life we all have those 'sliding door' moments when a decision that feels small and inconsequential at the time turns out to be big and affects you and your family for years. Choosing to shun the norm by not sending your children to school and opting for natural learning can be such a moment – a decision that was easy to make but that can determine your path for years. Personally, I see endless advantages for all the family in this lifestyle. Some are subtle, some instantly recognisable, and others only appreciated retrospectively.

ENDURING RELATIONSHIPS
No matter what your perspective or what your love language is, quality time has to be one of the best ways to nurture any relationship. When you have a child and then remove school from the equation, you have the most sublime perspective of the unfettered years stretching ahead of you. However your days and weeks

roll when you are with your children every day it would be hard for there not to be some positive outcomes from all that time spent together.

Relationships are crucial to being human. A healthy or toxic one can make or break a person. We live our lives more and more online, which brings with it a degree of disconnection from others, highlighting the importance of human relationships. Social isolation, loneliness, depression and anxiety are all at epidemic levels. Raising children to expect and experience good relationships potentially sets them on a course where they will seek and create the same quality relationships in their later lives. This is one of the less visible and long-term benefits of parenting with intent that is often only appreciated once the children have grown up.

If you live a life where respectful communication, being present, supporting those you love, and collaborating are all part of a normal relationship, the impact on your children will be long-lasting and hopefully flow down the generations. One of the best things you can do is to be a role model in your relationship with your child. Treat them how you wish to be treated yourself, and how you hope they will then treat others.

Most of us have historical hurts to resolve from relationships in our own childhoods. If you are parenting now without having dealt with these issues, then waste no time in delving in, forgiving, letting go and finding acceptance and love. Consciously addressing a generational continuation of hurtful behaviour, be it abuse, neglect or emotional unavailability, is the greatest gift you can offer your family. Heal yourself so the wounds and dysfunctional behaviour of your past are not passed on to your children. You may find yourself emulating what your parents did, or consciously creating the exact opposite of what you experienced as a child. This is emotional work that only you can do, in whatever way you choose, but the ripple effects are extensive, passing the benefits onto those around you now and the next generation.

I find it heartening to see the growth in each generation where this happens and can only wonder at the honest and meaningful relationships our children have and the positive possibilities for their offspring.

When I reflect on bringing up my children, I see relationships as being at the heart of our existence. They are the focal point of life – otherwise what are we here for? Our best learning and growth happens within our relationships, be it with children, a partner, neighbours, family, friends or colleagues. Relationships provide a mirror to our true self. Ask yourself if you are feeling triggered by someone's behaviour. If so, you can be sure that there is a part of you that needs work around this exact issue. Being grateful for our connection with others and looking at the gifts they bring into our lives can be easily practised with our dearest ones, our children. Other relationships can be more challenging, but parenting is a safe and loving place to gain experience and wisdom in being a better person so that the benefits can then flow out into other relationships.

> **THE BENEFIT OF STRONG RELATIONSHIPS**
> Being an integral part of our children's lives as they developed was an honour. It also afforded me great insight into how they coped with

change and stress, new experiences, and difficult situations. My deep knowledge of each of my children served us all well as they grew. It meant I could offer insights and help with more certainty of their response. Parents not engaged in natural learning have this connection too, but I found that by being present for most of their days I was able to observe the majority of influences they were open to. I did not miss six or seven hours a day, five days a week, of their experiences and interactions because they were at school. We dealt with issues as they arose and in a way that was respectful for them. Whatever was a priority for them was allowed to be a priority. No 'more important' agenda took precedence, especially not schoolwork. Their emotional selves were given attention, no matter how that manifested itself. I was present for all the big moments and available to support them when needed. I have no doubt this helped them by contributing towards their emotional security and giving them great freedom to explore away from me as they grew, knowing the solidity of our relationship and home life were a constant.

Rich and enduring relationships with young adult children are rewarding and come as a satisfying and sometimes unexpected bonus from active parenting. You and your child each know, at some level, the hours and the years of unconditional love and time that went into building and nurturing your relationship. Even though parenting is usually a labour of love, the solid relationships that emerge after a childhood of natural learning are what job satisfaction feels like at its very best.

SELF-AWARENESS

Many of the benefits of spending a childhood playing and following your own flow within the security of a family are psychological. The emotional, spiritual and mental advantages of such an upbringing can be long-lasting and profound. Letting a child follow their heart and interests as they grow, and supporting this process, discussing it and accepting it for what it is, increases the child's sense of self and their awareness of who they are. Knowing yourself and then loving and accepting yourself is a life's work for many of us yet can be a regular part of growing up for a child. As Socrates said, 'To know thyself is the beginning of wisdom.'

One of the things that develops in a young child is their understanding of themselves as a separate entity from you, with their own traits, behaviours and feelings. If you can articulate and celebrate their differences, their uniqueness and their special essence of self, then they are released from a swathe of debilitating and time-wasting emotions, and any self-doubt and self-loathing will hopefully be minimised. Many adults can trace an insecurity back to a comment made to them as a child. Their self-belief is affected, and they give themselves messages such as 'I can't sing' or 'I am no good at art/sport.' An offhand comment from a peer, a teacher or a parent can emotionally scar a person who will then carry that belief with them and act it out like a prophecy. Having the awareness and the confidence to be yourself is vital to be able to deflect judgements like this.

Building and supporting self-awareness in a young child is one of the most important jobs a parent can do. Often it is a relatively easy, continuous process that consists of listening to your child, appreciating them as they are, and letting them be who they were born to be. You don't need to mould them into anyone else. They have their own blueprint and direct the process of growing up instinctively. Your parenting is about helping them build up a story of who they are by affirming them and the choices they make. There are plenty of opportunities to reinforce a person's sense of worth without offering empty positive platitudes. If something is important to your child, then it is important. If something is worthy of them spending time and energy on, then it is worthy. A parent can learn to see this in their child and accept and love it with no hidden agenda of changing it or developing it to suit their own expectations. If you are one of the biggest influences in their childhood, there is a good chance their sense of self will be solidly embedded by the time they hit puberty and are out in the world more.

THINGS YOU CAN SAY TO OTHERS TO HELP BOOST THEIR CONFIDENCE AND SENSE OF SELF

- I can see that you love doing that.
- I understand that is frustrating/challenging/ exciting for you.
- What do you need right now?
- You are a fast runner/ a high climber/ a speedy skater.
- I can see that makes you feel sad/angry.

- Is there anything I can do to help you?
- I'm here.
- You have put a lot of work into that project.
- You rock!
- I love you just how you are.
- What would you like to do?
- I'm listening.
- What do you feel like playing/eating/reading?
- What's going on for you?
- I really appreciate you/your time/your hugs/your help.
- Thank you.

Recognising emotions is a part of learning naturally about yourself, but it is not something often found on a school curriculum. Emotional literacy requires years of practice in a safe environment. It needs to be demonstrated ('I feel so sad that our cat died'), supported ('I can see how frustrated you are right now') and explained ('I feel so hurt when you hit me'). Being able to talk about your emotions is one of the many paving stones you can provide for your child on their road to self-awareness. Talking about your emotions is no different to learning how to walk and talk. Naming feelings and expressing them is a skill to be modelled, discussed and celebrated.

A strong sense of self and an acceptance of self can help to avoid or lessen comparisons with others and the ensuing low self-esteem that can bring. By supporting your child, you can equip them to withstand the onslaught from peer pressure, potential bullying and later, the side effects of social media that may feature in a young person's life. If a child can learn to be confident in who they are, no matter how different they feel or act, this will set them up well in life.

Having a robust sense of self means knowing yourself well: what you are good at, how you enjoy spending your time, what causes you stress, and your personality traits. The focus on the individual has its limitations, however. We have seen how the cult of the individual has failed the human race miserably. We are now seeing a trend of turning back to community and connection, be it within a family, with neighbours, work colleagues or friends, as we remember how much we need each other. The family can be at the hub of this connectivity, providing a solid foundation for children as they discover their place in the world.

A secure childhood where each individual is valued for themselves and the gifts they bring to the world has produced some fine examples of young people with positive self-worth. This, in turn, usually means they have more time to pursue their interests fully and to help others, to give back and to take their place as positive contributing members of society.

TAKING THE TIME THAT IS NEEDED

Natural learning is about letting your child follow what they want to do, when they want to do it and for as long as it takes them. It is easy to underestimate the amount of time a young child can spend on one single game or project. Letting children take the time they need for any activity is an important parenting practice, and embarking on natural learning can give you the perfect opportunity to experience and support your children in this.

Giving children the time to finish what they are doing (that is, the time they tell you they need, and do need) is important. Learn to let them do things in their own time and to work to their own schedule. Letting children finish gives value to what they are doing – the game or the project. It gives value to them as learners and pursuers of an interest. If there is little hope in finishing something, why even begin? A child will feel empowered as a learner when they see that what they are doing or reading or playing is valued by the adults around them.

In a busy family this can seem impossible and of course there will be times when it is. However, as a parent you can minimise the times a child has to pack up or stop by taking their activities seriously and seeing the value in them. Perhaps you can leave a note or take a photo to remind them of what they were doing, or let them take it with them if you have to go out.

> **HOW MUCH TIME?**
> Early on I was impressed by the amount of time a four-year-old could spend on a single game or activity, before realising how much the school system had conditioned me to forget what children are capable of and what they needed to flourish. It seems that the three little people in my life all valued sticking at one activity, one game or one project and seeing it out. As a busy multi-tasking parent and a 'Jane-of-all-trades', this seemed astounding to me at first, but I quickly got used to it as I saw how incredibly focused the kids could be when they were left to finish in their own time. It did mean that we were nearly always the last to

leave the museum, the swimming pool, playground or library, and I needed to be endlessly patient waiting for them to finish.

I quickly saw the benefit of letting them finish what they were doing. It meant that a game or project could go on for a whole 12-hour day, for five or six consecutive days and nights, weeks or even months. I was acutely aware of this when school-going friends came to play and every half hour or so they would ask, 'What shall we do now?' My natural learners would look confused and say that they were still doing whatever they were engaged in and would be for a long time yet. I know if I am in the middle of a project and that creative energy is flowing, the last thing I want is to be interrupted and have to keep restarting, especially in someone else's timeframe. Why should children be any different?

Leaving children to finish things in their own time helps them develop attributes of concentration, persistence, resilience, determination and focus – all highly desirable qualities in any young student or employee. For a child to be able to trust that when they start something, they will be supported until they finish it, is a game-changer – they know they can continue for as long as they want and can trust that what they are doing will be valued. Regardless of whether the task requires long periods of quiet, calm creativity or raucous, messy, noisy games, the child will usually show focus and commitment to the activity. As the parent, having an awareness of the child's different needs for various activities can encourage you to help resource them well, as you know the task is unlikely to be abandoned after five minutes.

Letting children take the time they need also extends to 'down time', when they may consider themselves to be bored. Boredom is currently seen as the 'bad boy' by many parents. But from boredom creativity can spring. When you see a child sitting quietly, swinging, doodling or doing what looks like a mindless activity, don't be alarmed because this can be the perfect mental space for ideas to arrive. Creativity needs space, it even needs boredom to be able to grow. Creativity is a big deal; it is what drives many humans, colouring our world and our lives in numerous ways. The clothes we wear, the cars we drive, every building we enter and the food we eat are products of a creative process. It is an unseen force that drives us and in many ways defines our world. It is the ultimate expression of who we are.

The creative spark we are all born with is a strong life force, no matter how it is expressed. Creativity cannot be constricted to a timeframe, it cannot be scheduled. Taking the time you need when the inspiration strikes is a pure joy that many of us do not get to experience in our busy, modern lives. Natural learning creates the perfect time to foster creativity in a child, letting them see the worth of their own imagination and self-expression.

Supporting a child to explore their own creativity is often not about the outcome so much as the journey. For example, if a child is working on something or creating something, it doesn't necessarily mean that the end result has to be used or valued in a particular way. Often once a creative project is finished or made, then it has served its purpose. The learning may be complete, whether it is food preparation, sewing, painting, a Lego or sand creation.

Natural learning brings more quality time into your lives, which will hopefully provide you and your children more time for creative, innovative and productive pursuits. Understanding that my children needed to be allowed time to finish what they were engaged with was for me a big learning curve. It reminded me to be open and to accept all possibilities that the children presented.

GETTING THE SLEEP YOU NEED

Natural learning gives you all the chance to improve your health outcomes by allowing enough time to get the sleep you and your children need. When you become a parent, you soon realise it is a round-the-clock job. Parenting at night by providing an emotionally secure environment where you continue to meet a child's needs is just as important as the time you put in during the daylight hours. If you dedicate your weeks and years full time to your offspring, the benefits will quickly emerge. Giving up a timetable of early mornings for your family means your children (and hopefully you) can get the sleep needed to function optimally – a life with no alarm clocks. Good sleep is being recognised more and more as crucial for brain growth, healthy hormone function, the immune system and positive mental health.

Co-sleeping with babies and young children is another part of parenting that is common in natural learning circles. It is only in relatively recent times that crying babies were seen as 'naughty' or as 'exercising their lungs', and parents were often told that babies should not be picked up or comforted. Sleep programmes continue to be popular in our culture as the parents' needs are put before those of their baby. A young child is often not seen as a vulnerable, emotional human, but as disobedient and needing to be 'trained'. A baby or young child crying in distress, whether they are feeling afraid, alone, frustrated or hungry, is communicating in the only way they can. Surely as a parent or caregiver your job is to meet that need quickly and lovingly? A baby or young child needs to know that they are loved and someone they trust is there for them all day and all night, not just when it suits the adult.

Caregiving is a full-time job that demands much of you, and lack of sleep is a hazard of the job. But its effects can possibly be minimised by following your own natural schedule. Going to bed and to sleep can be another natural, loving part of the day for all concerned – if as a parent you have no expectations, no time schedule and are happy to let your baby lead the way. Is it your goal to have your child grow up knowing that sleep is a welcome and healthy part of life? Then practising respectful parenting during the night too is a necessity which will then contribute to their overall wellbeing, giving them both plentiful sleep and emotional security.

THE WONDERS OF CO-SLEEPING

In our family going to bed and to sleep was always a naturally enjoyable time for the kids. When they were young it meant cuddling up in bed with me and reading. Because they slept with us, until they decided to sleep alone, our nights were peaceful and settled. The benefits of the security they experienced, the ensuing long sleep with a natural wake up must have contributed to their general wellbeing.

Once they chose to sleep in their own rooms, the kids mostly developed a late-night rhythm, getting involved in a creative project and savouring the quiet house. They would then sleep late in the morning, ensuring they got the rest they needed. As they grew, they would sleep outside in a hammock or on the trampoline or experiment with the hours they kept to see how it felt. Going away on holidays was easy and hardly affected their sleep. As long as one parent was there, they would tuck in and nod off on a friend's floor, in a cabin, a tent or out under the stars.

Mornings were slow, quiet, sleepy times where each would rise, make their breakfast and drift into their day. I learned to savour that time and to use it wisely to meet some of my own needs. I am convinced that the plentiful amount of sleep they consistently got went a long way to helping them stay so healthy. The lack of stress around getting enough sleep was removed from the equation while also providing a learning opportunity for the kids to understand how a lack of sleep feels after a big weekend away on a camp, or on sleepovers with friends for several nights.

Many natural learners report similar scenarios, where children choose when and where they sleep and for how long. This makes sleeping just another part of their lives and will hopefully lead to a positive, life-long relationship with sleep.

SLEEP SHUFFLING

At 16 years, during lockdown, Charlie set himself a challenge to change his sleep schedule an hour a day. Over a few weeks he shifted to a completely opposite routine to me; he went running at 2am and was cooking dinner when I woke up in the mornings, giving us each a separate and complete run of the property while awake. I viewed this as a continuation of childhood exploration and saw the learning that arose for him.

Playing with sleep and learning through sleep are another part of life that can be explored by a child, given the time and opportunity to do so. Providing full time parental support to your natural learner is centred around the basics of a good life, where sleep is a priority for well being.

EATING WELL

Food is an important part of family life – whether it is a challenging necessity or if food preparation provides hours of creative expression. Being home-based full time can mean eating well becomes an unintentional side effect.

Although healthy eating is obviously not restricted to natural learners, being home-based can mean having more time to grow, harvest, preserve, prepare and cook quality food. Compared to parents managing food in a full-time working lifestyle, this can be a huge bonus, with many health benefits. If you subscribe to the idea that 'food is our medicine' and we are what we eat, then the positive spin-offs from time spent preparing food are innumerable.

Having the time to eat well is more than enjoying long meals made with home-grown food. With more time and hopefully less stress, children can learn about their own food needs and preferences and don't have to eat under pressure. Once you factor in minimising doctor visits and sick days, improved mental health and fewer chances of long-term health issues, the potential side effects of being home-based and practising natural learning are exponential. Eating slowly, eating when you are hungry and eating with others are all known to have health benefits and can play a part in reducing stress, especially around food.

You can of course send kids to school with healthy food, as many parents do, but nothing beats homemade soup by the fire on a winter's day with the time to enjoy reading a book for an hour or so while you eat it. In a natural learning household, more time is available to prepare and eat real food, which in turn brings a deeper, holistic meaning to the idea of a 'healthy lifestyle'.

CREATING A CONNECTED COMMUNITY

As you walk this less conventional path, you have the opportunity to build a community of like-minded people who will become a vital support system and your everyday buddies – the equivalent of your work colleagues and classmates. Your community can take many forms –perhaps another family or a few neighbours. Even if you spend lots of time with school-going families who support you, there is something affirming and relaxing about having a group of people sharing a similar parenting experience.

Belonging to a group with a shared philosophy must

be a basic need of being human. No matter what other differences you may have with other natural learning families, knowing you share some of the same parenting issues is hugely reassuring. Being able to speak freely about your nine-year-old not being interested in writing, or the fact that your children are never awake until after 10am, are common among natural learners. Sharing stories of late-night adventures, toddlers working freely with knives, young children climbing up and playing on the house roof and ambitious creative enterprises are all met with supportive nods and heartfelt understanding.

Natural learning also means parents may need to be proactive in finding people for children to learn from or with. People in the community may become mentors and teachers, new relationships are formed, often intergenerational. Such interactions enrich all involved and serve to enhance the experience of natural learning, while building a community with people you may not otherwise come into contact with. The richness gained is multifaceted, for whenever you interact with others, you are being an advocate and a natural learning role model, which helps normalise and promote natural learning with people who may have never heard of it.

When you build relationships in a community, who can predict what magic may happen? While you are finding a tutor to take a pottery workshop, you may connect with someone who is isolated, or who has unhappy children and had never considered taking them out of school. I know that I have enjoyed involving our wider community in our lives whenever possible, smashing stereotypes, highlighting similarities, and strengthening those bonds of connection.

OUR TRIBE

We are lucky to be part of a supportive group of home educators in our area. Our lifestyles have a lot in common, which we relish, but it is the beliefs behind our life choices that bond us together and sustain us. We can share openly about our children without being judged or told to send them to school. Raising our children together in our metaphorical village is affirming and inspiring. I have greatly valued being able to hear how other parents talk to their children and learn about how they cope with problems their children raise, all while practising respectful parenting. One of the huge benefits of sharing our lifestyle with other families was the variety of activities we organised and ran within our group of like-minded people, something we still do today. For years we have participated in a forest school, had an annual market day, shared potluck dinners, organised games nights, as well as trips to rivers and beaches, and we've been skating, swimming and walking together. We book into exhibitions, shows and concerts as a group. Members of our group, including the children, run workshops and offer opportunities to learn harakeke (flax weaving), felting, ukulele, knot-tying, woodwork and printmaking. We have enjoyed 'restaurant' evenings where the children created, cooked and served the food. With the camps and the purely social times this added up to a busy and rich social life.

Natural learning provides a chance to design your own community to meet the needs of all your family. There is no limit or constrictions on how that may look. Whether your extended family or neighbours are your 'go to' people, or you attend national camps with hundreds of other natural learners, the possibilities of meaningful connection await you.

Chapter 3

BEING THE PARENT OF A NATURAL LEARNER

What would be useful to know before you decide to step into natural learning? You may be wondering if this is what you want for your children. One common scenario is that it just does not work out, for any number of reasons, no matter how much a parent wants to keep their children at home to roam freely. Coping with the demands of full-time parenting on the fringe of society can be messy, exhausting and sometimes just plain difficult. On the other hand, those years spent with the children at home will hopefully be filled with love, good times and heart-warming fun. Flexibility becomes a top priority. Being available to help your child, and always being willing to change and delay plans, will all stand you in good stead. You will come to regard your offspring as your best buddies and appreciate that they are the people you choose to hang out with.

TRANSITIONING FROM SCHOOL TO NATURAL LEARNING

You and perhaps your children may need to 'de-school'. This is a term commonly used to describe a transition from school to natural learning. It is a time when everyone involved can adjust with empathy and without expectations about what should be happening. It may include a time of research and discovery for parents or a period of trying a variety of different paths. A child may be exhausted or traumatised by school life and need to rest and stay home a lot. It could also be the time to find a place where you feel accepted by other families who share your vision.

The importance of giving yourself time to adjust, with kindness, to what is a huge life transition cannot be overrated. You may choose the natural learning route because your child has been at school and been unhappy, bullied or unsupported. If you are in the early stages of natural learning, the transition from early childhood education, kindy or daycare to a lifestyle that seems to have no parameters can feel strange and sudden. If the decision to educate your child at home has come primarily from you, your child may not be fully committed to the new way of learning. In each of these scenarios you all need time to adapt, to work out the new 'normal' and to develop routines and rhythms. A general rule of thumb in natural learning circles is that for every year a child has been at school they need a month to de-school, but this of course will vary from person to person.

TRUSTING THE PROCESS

Natural learning is all about trust – trusting that your child knows what is best for them, what they need to do and how long they need to be doing it for. Trusting them and also trusting the process are the biggest things for a parent to learn, or perhaps re-learn. You may instinctively want to step in to prevent them from failing or experiencing something you imagine can only have a negative outcome. Your own parents' attitudes and practice may be shaping these impulses, ingrained habits overriding your intuition. You may also have to compromise any needs and expectations you have for control, tidiness and cleanliness.

Trusting a young child to learn naturally means taking the accepted process of learning, the established norm, and twisting it on its head. You are called on to plunge bravely into relatively uncharted waters, to follow your heart and your deepest parental instincts. While doing this, you are also required to take into account different personalities, learning styles, body clocks, seasons, moods, weather, dynamics, personal growth, hormones (including your own) and the dozens of other things that affect us humans.

If you are conditioned by the school system into expecting to see set results and proof of your child's abilities within an external timeframe, then this will be an extraordinary journey for you to learn about stepping back and relinquishing control of the process. Learning is a private matter, a unique passage for each person that no other person can know the full extent of, or have any need to.

KEEP TRUSTING STORY

Ollie has been training to join the army since he was four years old. Seriously. His whole natural

> learning journey has basically been preparing him for this. I have had so many people say to me, 'How can you let him join the army when you are a pacifist?' I guess the only answer is I love and accept him for who he is and trust he will find his way in life as he always has. The reality is he is not me, nor even a mini me. He is his own person, and my job has always been to support him to become the best version of himself each day. He is currently at university completing a degree in nursing, with a future in the army still very much on the cards.

As you learn to trust your children and what they are called to do, you will hopefully relax and enjoy what they are doing more and more. Ironically, once you let go of the worry and the need to control your child's activities, you begin noticing the incredible learning taking place that was under your nose all the time. It can be a case of getting out of your own way and your children's way, while being observant and mindful of what is important to them.

BEING A PARENT FIRST – NOT A TEACHER

You do not have to be a teacher to educate your children at home, no matter what philosophy you follow. You do not even have to have done well at school yourself or to have enjoyed school. We live in an expert culture where teachers are one of the professions whose members are regularly placed on a pedestal by some. This means you could be fearful about your ability to educate your child, or believe you should be doing exactly what a teacher does in a school for the learning to qualify as 'education'.

I have often had people point out that I was a teacher, like many natural learning parents are, so I knew what to do. But as a natural learning parent, I have never 'taught' my children with anything I ever learned in my teaching degree. I didn't follow a curriculum or a timetable, and I never assessed their progress. I didn't have to control and organise large groups of students. I never had to plan or mark schoolwork or go to meetings. I didn't even have to create fancy wall displays. However, having been a teacher and having an insight into the system and what life in a busy classroom looks like has given me an advantage over other parents only in that it has taught me what I do not want for my children.

I know about the 1:30 classroom ratio and how that translates in terms of quality student time with an adult. I know about children lining up, sitting down, waiting for others to catch up, never quite catching up, being bored and being overwhelmed. I know about the time that is wasted waiting, with days of childhood passing in a flurry of busy, but essentially irrelevant work that the authorities have deemed necessary. I figured that whatever happened at home would be vastly superior to much of this, on so many levels.

I do not see natural learning as 'teaching' in the traditional sense. Natural learning is first and foremost about parenting. Your job is to parent your child with all your heart, to be there for them, listen to them, love them and trust them. Your role will quickly become dominated by meeting their needs and answering their incessant questions. You do not need to be a perfect parent, because you too are on a journey of discovery and will grow with your children. I fervently believe that every parent is doing the best they can with what they know at the time.

There is no definitive list of what qualities you need to be a natural learning parent because every family is different. The different personalities within the family, the way you interact and each person's changing needs demand an array of skills. The qualities I have brought to my natural learning style that have worked well with my own children may not work so well in another family. Your parental instincts and heart-centred acceptance are the mainstay in parenting with empathy.

ASSESSING THE RESPONSIBILITY

Parents educating their children at home may feel that the sole responsibility for educating your child rests on your shoulders and yours alone. Their education can seem like a Herculean task, sometimes filling you with self-doubt and fear of failure. Questioning your decision to keep your children from school is constantly in the minds of many parents, weaving through the children's upbringing and resurfacing at times of change or stress. You will never know what could have been, either way. Would your children have blossomed at school? Are you letting them down, by offering a 'sub-standard' option? Will they turn around as a young adult and be full of recrimination for how they missed out? The same possibilities may arise for those who have spent 13 years at school – what could their childhoods otherwise have been like? What different lives would they be living at 18 years of age had they been natural learners?

When you are going it alone there is no system to blame, no teacher or school yard bullies to point the finger at if things go wrong. You can't excuse a lack of learning or bad behaviour on a terrible principal, a dumbed down curriculum or a system under pressure with not enough funding. At the end of the day, you are the biggest influence on your children, and you get one chance to give it your all.

This may all sound terrifying but know that you are not alone, and it is perfectly normal to be constantly assessing how things are working out for you and your children. It is only natural to feel overwhelmed with doubt when the common narrative is so vastly different from natural learning and is so regularly discussed and the only available measure for 'success'. School is usually seen as the only option in our society's educational system and there are no other measuring tools. With no other choices, it is a common trap to believe that the existing option must surely be reliable, effective and successful. Right?

> **HAPPY KIDS MOST IMPORTANT**
>
> The responsibility of educating my children did weigh heavily on me at times. This was especially evident at the beginning of our journey, or when the children entered different stages of development, such as puberty, or if I was feeling vulnerable or overwhelmed in myself. Generally, these times were minimal as the kids themselves demonstrated such contentment with their lives. My experience of teaching, coupled with talking to school-going children who visited our home regularly, was a constant source of reassurance that our kids were having a balanced and fulfilling life as natural

> learners. It was obvious that they were happy, and this was often enough reason to pause, observe and know I was doing the right thing.

WHAT IF IT'S NOT RIGHT FOR US?

No matter how appealing raising your children this way may sound, it may not be the best thing for you, for your child, or your family. Part of the mindset of being child-centred is being open to doing what works best, for your children and for you. This may mean your children go to school. Many natural learners dip in and out of school and some families have one child who prefers school, especially once they are teenagers. However, it's not all about the kids. Making the decision to follow the natural learning path needs to be made not only by the children but by the adult/parents/caregiver who will be spending the majority of the time with the kids. Maybe you start the natural learning journey and change your mind. Or maybe you prefer to go out to work or need more time away from your kids than is possible while facilitating natural, home-based learning.

I have often noticed that parents of school-going children can be divided into two groups when it comes to school holidays. There are those who love the school holidays, plan for them, cherish them and never want them to end. When I see these parents, I know they would love to have their children around more and would possibly thrive as natural learners. On the flip side there are parents who dread the holidays or find them stressful and count down the days until their kids return to school, breathing a sigh of relief when term starts. Keeping the children in school could be the best option in this case, where everyone's needs are met and weekends and holidays provide enough quality time together, while maintaining your sanity as a parent.

If you are uncertain about taking your kids out of school, look at the reasons why you are unsure about educating at home. If it's a question of the time commitment, there may be other ways to be actively involved in their education while keeping your children in school. You can be a natural learner in your heart while it may not be feasible in your family right now. The list of reasons for engaging with natural learning given below is not exhaustive, but it might enable you to see where the desire is coming from and to clarify whose needs will be met through natural learning.

REASONS FOR NATURAL LEARNING
- Missing your kids and wanting more time as a family.
- Disagreeing with elements of the school system – religious beliefs, core values, wider societal issues.
- Not liking the teacher or principal of your child's school
- Having an unhappy child, who is not enjoying school
- Meeting other natural learners and feeling that you 'should' do this too
- Thinking you could do a better job than school
- Liking the idea of being the largest influence on your children
- Wanting to have a flexible timetable so you can travel

- Simplifying your life
- Having children with particular needs that cannot be met in school
- Seeing natural learning as an easy option
- Having a desire to live outside the predominant, mainstream culture

You may have a strong need, maybe wanting more time with your children, that you think natural learning will meet yet feel unsure about actually embarking on it. This may mean finding other ways to meet that need, or bring more of what is missing into your life, while your children go to school. This could be accomplished with better time management, making sure you are fully available out of school hours, prioritising quality time together, removing time sapping activities (like screen time) from your lives or taking mental health days off together. Parenting is a tough job, so if school works best for your family, then don't feel regretful about a life missed, but create the life you desire with the time you have available, focusing on the activities you all love best. If you need to work to support your family and cannot have the luxury of having them at home full time, then enjoy the times you do have, celebrating the wonderfulness of who you all are and creating a rich family life that complements school.

TIME AND SACRIFICE

Spending so much time with your children can be viewed as a huge plus, as long as it is loving, mostly positive and supportive of who they are. A big consideration is the time you will get to spend with your children and whether this is advantageous to everyone involved. Consider the amount of time and energy that you are required to give to your offspring. If you embark on parenting in this way, you are looking at years and years of full-time, seven-days-a-week, 24-hours-a-day work. The wonderful moments of love and fun we experience while raising children are more numerous with natural learning, and so also is the continuous daily grind.

The sacrifices that may be required will become apparent as you settle into the natural learning lifestyle. Do you receive enough emotional support from your kids? Do you have enough mental stimulation? Are you able to set boundaries with them as they mature and can understand you need time to focus on other things? You may need to set the kids up with an activity, for instance, so you can make a phone call or have a shower without being interrupted. If you have expectations of achieving many other things while you raise natural learners, then you may be disappointed. This could become an issue, creating resentment or a sense of failure along with a feeling of losing your own identity in the domesticity of life as a parent. Juggling work, hobbies, your own 'down' time and social life all need to be considered. After all, it is your life too.

We often imagine before a baby arrives that our lives won't change so much just because of a new person in the family. Luckily hormones usually kick in after the birth and hopefully a great love affair with your baby begins. This period is usually the beginning of you as a parent letting go of expectations you may have had before the baby arrived. If you are going to venture into natural learning, then having two parents on board and perhaps even your extended family is a definite bonus, as is a supportive community of friends. I know several women who had children but were desperate to return to work and felt a mix of emotions about parenting not being enough for them. Make sure you are all enjoying life and if things change then roll with it and accept it with grace, knowing you are doing your best.

Giving years to raising your children full time can also be viewed as a sacrifice for some parents. A common narrative about being a full-time parent is having to forgo your career, or the inability to save money or purchase expensive big-ticket items.

A PRIVILEGE, NOT A SACRIFICE

I hesitate to use the word 'sacrifice' about parenting full-time, as for me it was a privilege and honour to spend so much time with my children. I could have pursued a career, or we could have owned a bigger or more expensive house, but I was lucky to have felt the joy and the importance of being with my kids – and that was priceless.

Being out of the paid workforce for 15, 20 or more years could mean the end of a promising career. Ageism, rapidly changing technology, jobs and work attitudes can trigger a fear about future security. If you choose to commit to raising your family full time, does this feel like a sacrifice or a personal choice that empowers you and fills your heart? Seeing it as a sacrifice implies there may be some disappointment further down the track, which may be compounded when your children finally fly the nest. Children will most certainly pick up on your feelings if you feel you are sacrificing your time to be with them. I have heard parents articulate this to children too, which no doubt stems from frustration on the parents' part. There is possibly an expectation of certain behaviours or outcomes if you tell them, 'I have given up my career to look after you.'

Meanwhile full-time parents are activists, making a stand for job satisfaction and raising awareness of the importance of parents in a child's life and education. In a culture of daycare centres and full-time working parents, spending whole decades of your life parenting full time is often seen as quirky, boring and even unnecessary. Your 'sacrifice' will be highlighted by society's perception of you, by the media and of course by family and friends as they project their own fears onto you and your chosen lifestyle.

However, you are not living in a vacuum. As natural learners you can fully engage with life on all levels, even with your children alongside. You can keep up with trends, develop business ideas, study and work. Perhaps working online from home and combining natural learning and a career is workable for your family. Parents who engage in natural learning often both work part time and can juggle the whole family in a multitude of creative ways.

EMOTIONAL LABOUR AND SELF-CARE

Before embarking on the natural learning lifestyle, consider how you will nurture your own mental and emotional health. This is something that also needs to be attended to during your parenting journey. In amongst all the cuddles and kisses you receive, parenting can be a hard, relentless and thankless job which can easily lead to feelings of loneliness and isolation. With natural learning you are giving to your kids all day and often through the night as well. It is an intense job, the impact of which should be carefully considered.

If you think too deeply about the repercussions of natural learning, you may feel overwhelmed. However, it does pay to take a moment every now and then to check in with how everyone is doing. This includes how you, the parents, are coping. Are you getting enough exercise and staying physically healthy? Do you feel positive about your life? Do you have a friend who accepts you and listens to you? Do you get the support you need from the other parent, your immediate and wider family and adults in your life? How are you faring mentally? Do you know what you need to wind down and relax, or to organise and get things done?

Be aware also that you, your children and your circumstances will change over the years. Natural learning offers the chance to start living in the present. Children growing up marks the passing of the years like nothing else. Each birthday reminds us to enjoy what we have today, for who knows what tomorrow brings? Try to keep the enjoyment in your lifestyle, and to contain any worry to what is happening in the present.

Emotional and mental labour are commonly accepted concepts now, highlighting the unacknowledged labour of many parents, especially women. Parenting may not yet be a fully valued occupation in our culture, but let's hope attitudes are changing. Natural learners can be at the forefront of this discussion, making the world aware of the benefits and advantages of full-time parenting. Raising your children well can also be a political statement, helping to pave a new path for those coming behind you while raising the profile and image of parenting.

THE MENTAL LABOUR

The first year I had the kids at home full time I got sick and was wiped out for weeks. I knew that this was some form of burnout and a signal to me to slow down and lose some of the expectations I had placed on myself. I instigated small, self-care type activities that could then increase as the kids got older. They ranged from having a 'question free time' after 8pm, which failed completely, to heading out alone for a walk in the morning and then eventually, weekends away with friends. When I first heard of 'emotional and mental labour' I instantly understood the terms and felt a great relief that there was a name for what parents have been doing for years. It felt like a small but significant recognition.

If you are committing to being a parent, especially as a natural learner, then be prepared for some intensity along with the good times. You are the world to your child, but you must give priority to your self-care – put the proverbial oxygen mask on yourself first so you can help care for your children. Take time to care for yourself in whatever way you need, no matter how small it may seem: a few minutes lying down, sitting with a cup of tea, reading a book, talking to a friend, getting dressed alone, having regular time out or a secret chocolate stash.

CAN YOU AFFORD TO BE A FULL-TIME PARENT?

A common response from parents wanting to take their kids out of school is, 'We can't afford it, we both need to work.' The cost of living is increasing faster than the average pay packet, which in many families has resulted in both parents needing to work. Yet more and more I see creative ways people are coping financially once they start a family. Both parents may work part time, for instance, some working from home or sharing childcare with others. Some families consider living in a different place, away from expensive cities, or sharing land with another family so they can raise their children out of school. To live more simply, or in a cheaper part of the country, sharing childcare, gardens, labour, cars or large appliances with other families may have more benefits than raising your children as a single-family unit possibly under financial pressure.

> ### HOW WE MANAGED FINANCIALLY
>
> People often ask how we were able to manage financially as a natural learning family. I was fortunate that my partner, their dad, was employed as a teacher and was happy to support me being at home with our children. Our house was not fancy or expensive, but it was home. Once the kids were older, I started teaching music privately at home, which I did for ten years. This supplemented our income and paid for extracurricular activities like dance, drama, Scouts and swimming lessons. However, we never had any spare money and lived simply. We have always had a large vege garden, we wore second-hand clothes and did clothes swaps

with our natural learning group, and we didn't buy lots of 'stuff' as we value experience over things. I was also constantly aware that the choices I was making were coming from a privileged place, as we live in Aotearoa New Zealand, owned a house and did not have any great hardships to contend with.

When the kids were 14, 12 and nine years old I took them on a big trip, where we spent nearly five months travelling. To do this I borrowed a large sum of money from the bank against our mortgage, as I knew it was 'now or never'. The children were growing up, which meant I could return to work in some form in the near future and pay the trip off. I feel lucky to have had access to a mortgage in the first place and the support to make this happen.

Children in a natural learning environment seem to be happy when they are with you, doing what they want. I felt that our children were accepting of our lifestyle and never wanted for anything. They also never asked for possessions. They were always grateful for birthday gifts and creative with what they already had. Although they all enjoyed owning things and were protective and careful with what they valued, I perceived that they didn't need or rely on material possessions. Their emotional security was more important. Money gives us the freedom to make choices and removes the stress of worrying about our basic needs and providing for our family. An excess of money however is not necessary to raise children who are well adjusted and secure.

Choosing to parent full-time is a huge commitment that will, hopefully, have equally large benefits for everyone. Once you have established what your needs are and can focus on others then life will flow more easily, your own enjoyment spilling over to the other members of the family. Remembering that natural learning is about the adults as much as the children should help balance a full-time life together.

Chapter 4

PHILOSOPHY, VALUES AND FAMILY CULTURE

Natural learning is not an isolated belief nor is it a single ideology. It is a diverse, holistic educational philosophy that is formed by and reflects your lifestyle and that of the community in which you live. There are many theories and principles that are complementary to natural learning, fitting in easily with the whole lifestyle. The foundation of your parenting and therefore the organic way your children will learn is built on your beliefs, your values and the culture you build within your family. Children are learning all the time, instinctively, whether you like it or not. The question to ask is, 'What exactly are they learning?'

COMPLEMENTARY IDEOLOGIES
Playcentre
Playcentre is an early childhood organisation, unique to Aotearoa New Zealand, with over 500 centres throughout

the country. Similar to the Montessori philosophy of self-directed learning, Playcentre encourages child-led learning experiences while supporting parents who are recognised as the first educators of their children. Training is provided and parents can run sessions while learning alongside their children. Playcentre has been a huge inspiration for me. For years I called the natural learning we were doing 'Playcentre at home' and have heard other natural learning parents say the same.

We belonged at different times to three Playcentres around the country, and each provided a strong sense of community. I saw first-hand how play-based learning operates and was inspired by the way children and their play were treated with respect. I loved the way a child's interests were supported with resources, and how help was given when asked for, with extension ideas sometimes offered. I learned from observing an adult actively listening to a child, then following up on their questions. I was intrigued to see how much time a four-year-old could concentrate and dedicate to one project when not interrupted. The learning I gained during these years at Playcentre laid solid foundations for my own parenting practice. This grounding in early childhood education empowered me as my children's first educator and gave me the confidence to carry on the same approach at home. So much of the way I have parented was influenced by people I had met and interactions I had seen at Playcentre.

Nonviolent Communication

When meeting a child's needs through natural learning, the principles of nonviolent communication are useful to be aware of and employ. Nonviolent communication

(NVC), sometimes called compassionate communication, was developed by the American psychologist and teacher Marshall B. Rosenburg. It helps you reframe how you express yourself and hear what others are telling you. Within a parenting context, NVC shows how to actively listen to your child and helps you understand why you may get upset in some circumstances. NVC is based on the idea that when someone is behaving in a way that can be seen as negative (for instance, angry, frustrated, upset, mean, scared), they have a need that is not being met. NVC enables you to identify that need and work out ways to ensure the need is met. It can be a life-changing way to communicate and not just with your children. I highly recommend reading Marshall B. Rosenburg's book, Nonviolent Communication: A Language of Compassion, or attending an NVC workshop in person or online.

I have been lucky to be surrounded by friends who parent in a similar way to me and who are also proficient practitioners of NVC in everyday life. They have helped me see NVC in action and given me concrete examples of how to phrase statements, ask questions, express myself and help my communication with my children. A seemingly simple change of language can have immediate effect, as those you are talking to do not feel threatened, blamed or shamed in any way. The dynamics of a tense relationship can alter dramatically for the better by adopting effective communication such as NVC.

Attachment Parenting

Attachment parenting is based on a kind and respectful relationship between an infant and their caregiver and is practised widely within natural learning communities. Attachment parenting usually involves talking to your children respectfully, co-sleeping, breastfeeding until child-led weaning takes place, baby and toddler wearing/carrying and parenting babies and children to sleep.

The Emmi Pikler approach is an important influence of attachment parenting. Emmi Pikler was an Austrian born pediatrician who worked in Hungary and set up an orphanage after World War Two. Her beliefs and research showed how the relationship between an infant and their caregiver is most important. She believed that a strong attachment, based on respectful communication, is vital and influences both physical and mental development in young children. Emmi strongly advocated for letting babies and young children learn at their own pace through uninterrupted child-led play.

Attachment parenting has much in common with natural learning as they both include meeting your child's needs as soon as possible, as lovingly as possible and for as long as needed. This has been the crux of my parenting and therefore the essence of natural learning for us.

TRUE INDEPENDENCE

I have always valued independence. Before I had children, I thought that if you managed to teach your children to be independent as babies that would make them so as adults. But as soon as I gave birth and held my daughter Hannah, I realised that it was the complete opposite; if I was there for my babies every second, meeting their needs and never giving them reason to feel scared, alone, desperate, wondering, unloved, disempowered or unimportant, then it would lead to them feeling emotionally secure, happy, confident and eventually, when they are ready, independent.

Moving into independence is not a process that can be defined by age, only by stage of development. Personalities and individual experiences will determine how much a child needs you and for how long. Within our natural learning community, for instance, we have seen girls becoming independent earlier than boys. Allowing children to decide for themselves when they are ready to move into their own bed or their own room or to venture out alone is a stress-free and nurturing way to parent.

IN THEIR OWN TIME
In our family Hannah was the most independent of our children. She was happy to sleep in her own room from about the age of seven, but she would still occasionally appear in our room, quietly in the middle of the night up until puberty. Ollie was strongly attached to me, even during the day. He would be concerned, for example, about where I was in the public library and needed reassurance that I would come back to him after choosing my books. He slept in our room until he was ten and a half, then within the same week he moved into his own room and announced he was cycling on his own to the local library. A sudden shift had occurred inside him but we could only see the outward reflection of this.

These developmental markers helped show me how

emotional attachment is key to our sense of security and happiness, but also to emerging independence. Your child's journey to independence may continue over many years. With natural learning, meeting the needs of your children becomes your main occupation as a parent. Being aware of your child's changing needs through each stage of development is key to guiding them towards independence. The needs of a 14-year-old will look different to those of a four-year-old. They call on you, as a parent, to have their back in new ways at different stages, and the best outcome will emerge from supporting them. Independence does not mean they will never need you. I know I will still be needed and always be available as a parent, but I am happy to have such independent children.

ALTERNATIVE EDUCATIONAL MODELS

Some well-respected alternatives to state schools share similarities with natural learning in terms of their underpinning philosophy, and could be an option for those who don't want their children to go to school, but who are unable to have their children at home all day. Montessori schools, for example, offer a child-centred approach where students can work at their own pace and on whatever they choose. Rudolph Steiner/Waldorf schools offer a more spiritual perspective, a holistic focus on the whole person and a play-based curriculum, grounded in the natural world. For pre-school and primary-aged children, Reggio Emilia inspired schools offer child-centred, project-based learning with a self-guided curriculum.

In my natural learning circles, I know of several

instances where a parent or other adult (often an ex-teacher) runs a day-long programme one or more days a week for a group of students. The classes are funded by the parents, who have a day off (and could potentially use that time to work) while their children spend a day with peers in a class-type situation, engaged in a variety of activities. This could be a simple way to start a 'school' type model with minimal input.

FAMILY CULTURE

Your particular version of natural learning is like the particular version of your life. Each family has its own culture. Whatever your family culture is will be a part of how you parent and how you raise your children. Many things will have influenced what goes on in your home and how you choose to spend your time. Your extended and combined families, your cultural practices, political and religious beliefs will all influence your lifestyle. A family's culture will change as much as the people in the family do.

If you are mad about horses, then this will continue to be what your family does. Perhaps your family loves to surf, hunt, skate, read comics, make art, or play internet games. The way you live and how you spend your time and money are noted and absorbed by your children. What you give your attention to and what you talk about will affect your children. Whenever you react, when you change the tone of your voice or have a strong emotional reaction, perhaps becoming upset or angry, your children are noticing and collecting all this information, soaking it up and learning from what they see and hear.

However you spend your days and your years will be

the life that your children remember and be what shapes them. Your young children are constantly adopting your beliefs, your attitudes and behaviours.

> **YOUR FAMILY CULTURE**
> - What fun family activity do you all enjoy and could be used to identify your family culture? (For example, we all love to cycle, we all play musical instruments.)
> - What are the defining features of your family or household? Are you a blended family, or an only child? Do you live somewhere interesting?
> - Can you think of two or three words to best describe the collective group that is your family? (For example, kind, quiet, fun-loving, tidy, hilarious.)
> - What is your favourite way to share food together? What favourite meals do you all enjoy?
> - Do you have any regular family traditions? (For example, on birthdays and holidays.) What happens in your family when a child loses a tooth, or when a young person enters puberty, or becomes an adult?
> - Do you have a regular time for sharing daily news or family meetings?
> - Do you have a favourite song, a family story or a flag? (For example, we created a family coat of arms composed of a small image created by each family member)

These ideas can be adapted or adopted to help create

a sense of belonging and a feeling of togetherness as a family group. They may trigger a conversation that ends up introducing some new shared activities into your lives. They might prompt a memory of a family tradition that has lapsed or encourage older family members to share stories about their way of life in earlier days. You may take the above list at face value, read and tick each one off, and have plenty of your own special ideas to share. Your family is unique. By being conscious of your family culture in some ways, no matter how small, can enhance your children's sense of security and help to bond you together.

RULES

Family rules reflect what you value and place importance on. Rules that are adapted as part of how you live may be your beliefs manifested in physical form. For example, spiritual beliefs may mean you give thanks before eating. Do you have rules in your family, and if so, what are they? Are they edicts laid down by you, the adults, or shared agreements created by the whole family? Rules are an interesting topic to discuss as a family. Who makes them? When and how do they change? Who enforces them?

MINIMAL RULES

We had only two rules in our home, which were that musical instruments and board games only be used for their intended purpose. I felt strongly about these and was happy to remind the children of them. It was almost a joke that we had no other rules, yet the children picked up what was expected

> and accepted in our family by inference or through being modelled by others. We never expressly asked them to respect each other or us when speaking, but apart from childhood squabbles and sibling rivalry, it eventually happened naturally. There were no hard and fast rules about eating or sleeping or what had to be worn. Each child experimented and learned about these in their own way. Expectations may have been expressed but were not enforced in any way. I have no belief or interest in punitive, power-wielding parenting that causes a child to shrink.

As you work on living together as a family, you will need to keep updating things, and checking in with each other as to what is relevant and still enjoyed by everyone. An annual family brainstorm of intentions or goal-setting might work for your family. Children grow and change so quickly. A meeting like this can be a great impetus for change in everyone and in your family as a whole.

WHAT VALUES DO YOU LIVE BY?

Parents and caregivers have a huge influence on the children they are caring for and raising. Ask yourself what they are learning by watching you, listening to you and seeing the values you live your life from. We may be unaware of what our values are. We often operate on autopilot, reiterating ways that were programmed into us from our childhood. Maria Montessori said, 'We cannot give principles by teaching them but by prolonged social experience.' Natural learning offers a wonderful opportunity to stop and look at your own values and those you wish to honour more in your lives. It can be difficult to find the time to think about our values as busy parents.

I have been surprised by the feedback from my children about how much of me they absorbed. They love to talk about the values they have taken with them as they grow up, the things I did or said that clearly showed them what was important to me. I never felt I consciously taught them, or preached to them about what I believed, yet they have picked up much more than I had ever realised. With this in mind, it may be a good idea to consider your own and shared values as parents.

YOUR VALUES
- What values do you have from your upbringing? Your schooling?
- What values do you think your children will need to survive and thrive in the years ahead?
- What values do you see people needing to help heal the planet?
- When have you been the happiest and most fulfilled? Why was that? What was happening?
- What do you see as the meaning of life? For example, are you here to learn as much as possible, be financially successful, follow your dreams, do what makes you happy? What do you value that your kids will see and emulate?
- Do you remember, as a child, all the possessions and toys you had? Do you remember the TV you watched? Do you remember holidays, experiences, small gestures, time with parents and siblings and games you played?

Generating thoughts, awareness and discussion around what your life is based on can bring direction and meaning into your lives. It can also help bring about change. If you realise that you valued playing board games as a child, but never have time to play with your own children, this insight may be enough to instigate a change. If you think that growing food, building, hunting or foraging will be essential skills for your children, then you can devise related activities, adventures, classes or outdoor time into your week. Changing your focus and creating the outward manifestation of an inner value is empowering.

> **VALUES I HAVE SEEN REFLECTED IN MY CHILDREN**
> - A three-year-old breastfeeding his doll – attachment parenting, compassion
> - Organising a peace march – standing up for your beliefs, justice, service.
> - Busking to buy expensive Lego sets – financial independence
> - Not spending pocket money on junk food – saving money
> - Spending a birthday camping or tramping – adventure, connection to the natural world
> - Organising camps for younger natural learners – valuing community, leadership
> - Carefully removing spiders and their nests – compassion, care for natural world
> - Practising over and over to learn an instrument – perseverance, determination
> - Spending 12 hours inventing, designing and making a work of art – creativity

- Teaching yourself to do a headstand – persistence

Recognising your own values can be an interesting and rewarding exercise that can be revisited each year. Knowing your top three values can help you reset the way you spend your time. Like a light being shone on your very essence, knowing your values can be a catalyst for you to question what you are doing and saying while interacting with your family. Including children in discussions about what you believe and what you prioritise is a good way to show them they are valued members of your family group whose opinions are taken seriously.

Choosing core values as a family can be a fun and illuminating experience and open the way for some rewarding conversations. Here is a small list of some of my core values. It is by no means a definitive list. Check online to find more comprehensive lists of values, or write your own. Writing values onto cards that can then be used as a game for your family, prioritising them, choosing your top three, seeing how they may change over time and guessing other family members' top values.

Authenticity	Justice
Adventure	Kindness
Beauty and colour	Knowledge
Bravery	Love
Communication	Nature
Compassion	Optimism
Challenge	Patience

Community	Peace
Contribution	Persistence
Cooperation	Personal growth
Creativity	Pleasure
Curiosity	Respect
Determination	Responsibility
Family	Security
Friendships	Self-Respect
Fun	Service
Happiness	Simplicity
Health	Spirituality
Honesty	Trustworthiness
Humour	Wisdom
Integrity	

As an adult you can reflect on your upbringing and identify the values that were important to your parents, even if they were not aware of them. For instance, I have a friend whose mother's first comment about someone always refers to their physical looks – how beautiful, or not, they are. It has taken her years to feel good about herself and she still fields comments and criticisms from her mother. They say the apple doesn't fall far from the tree and this is so true in our offspring and easy to see in concrete terms when considering a list of values. I see parents either copying the way they were raised or intentionally doing the complete opposite, especially if they had a negative experience growing up themselves. Your values give your children something to follow and something to push against and question as they grow.

VISIBLE VALUES

When reading a novel with my children I would often have to stop and cry or rant about some social injustice or outdated misogyny (we read a lot of Enid Blyton). The kids would sit respectfully through this break in the story telling, waiting for the reading to resume. Now as young adults I can appreciate their own emotional openness and willingness to be vulnerable. I can hear them demanding justice and stepping up to voice opinions in public arenas. There was a period of time when driving in town that the boys would spot a fast-food outlet and pretend to blow it up. There was no subtlety about where this came from and I was highly amused by their loyal, yet violent, adoption of my blatantly expressed values.

While you may be focusing on setting up a physical environment for learning in your home and arranging classes and play dates, be reminded that there are many unseen influences on your children that come from you. Taking the time to focus on what you value and believe will have as big an effect on your children as anything else. Creating the life you want through your words, thoughts and actions applies as much as ever when raising children. Life can be about what you are being as much as what you are doing.

Chapter 5

CREATING A LEARNING ENVIRONMENT

So, you have decided to jump in and embrace the life of natural learning. Perhaps it comes as a gentle transition from your involvement with early childhood education. No matter how you came to the decision to commit to natural learning, some simple strategies will help ease the way forward emotionally, mentally and practically. Setting out with conviction, surrounding yourself with like-minded people, and establishing support networks are some of the best ways to lay solid foundations for the years of education ahead. Remember too that your children will generally be fine as long as you are, so focus on what you need to maintain your confidence and to stay healthy.

MAKING IT LEGAL
First things first. Before you can start officially as a natural learning family, you need to ensure you are legally permitted to educate your children at home. Each country

has its own laws in this regard, and many countries outlaw it altogether.

In Aotearoa New Zealand a child must attend school from the age of six unless they are granted an exemption. Any child who is educated at home must have an exemption. To gain an exemption you need to undergo an initial permission-granting process, followed by a continued, legally binding agreement between you (the parents or caregivers) and the Ministry of Education. The application is made online and requires you to show how you will fulfil the educational needs of your child, as defined by the Ministry of Education. You will need to 'satisfy the Ministry that your child will be taught at least as regularly and as well as they would be in a registered school'.

You will be required to supply a substantial amount of information in your application, but once permission is granted, it covers your child until they turn 18 or go to school. The exemption application asks for your philosophy, a list of resources, a timetable, the subjects to be covered, and an explanation of your assessment methods. If you are planning to follow a natural learning path, it may prove challenging to write an exemption with integrity, showing how you can fit your educational intentions into the mould provided, while still showing clearly and honestly how your child is to be educated.

Making an application for exemption and openly explaining what you intend to do is an opportunity to create change in the education system by spreading the knowledge of natural learning. Your explanation becomes a type of political activism, which many applicants choose to engage with, advocating for natural learning to be an accepted educational path by conferring it with recognition and status. Some friends engaged with natural learning have even met with ministry officials to explain what natural learning is, hoping for some understanding that can then be reflected in the exemption process. Engagement with the Ministry is ongoing, and results vary depending on the staff handling your case. Interestingly, here in Aotearoa New Zealand, we have many natural learning 'refugees' – families from other countries who are making the most of the opportunity to educate their own children while they are living here.

As I see it, there are two main approaches you can take when applying for an exemption. The first is to try to introduce some awareness of what natural learning is, by using the term, explaining the philosophy behind it, and recording examples of the learning your child experiences. It's easy to feel strongly about your desire to practise natural learning, which can seem at odds with having to conform to the mainstream system. Applying for an exemption is the perfect opportunity to express your thoughts.

The second approach is to 'speak the language' of mainstream education and tick the boxes required to gain your exemption. If you are not trying to change the system, then you can choose to engage in this way and provide the officials with what they need to satisfy their requirements. The gap between formal education and natural learning is slowly closing, however. Greater attention is now being given to 'inquiry-based learning', which has similarities to natural learning. The concepts of a 'child-led' or 'play-based' curriculum and 'self-directed' learning or inquiry are now readily understood by those in education, while also representing the reality of how your children are learning. Many natural learners write an exemption application that is a mix of these two approaches.

The process of applying for an exemption may also help cement your beliefs about natural learning and show you just how much your child is learning at home. If you are starting out, the application can help guide you in the direction you want to explore and clarify why you have chosen this route. It may be interesting to look back on this document in later years, as you will inevitably make changes over time to how your children are educated.

FINDING YOUR TRIBE
When you adopt the lifestyle of natural learning, you live on the edge of the mainstream. You are likely to encounter some vocal family members, friends and even complete strangers who disapprove of the choice you have made and who believe it is their duty to explain that you are putting your children at a disadvantage.

It truly does take a village to raise a child, and embarking on natural learning is the perfect time to find your own, fringe-dwelling tribe. Connecting with people who share your philosophy will be important, especially as you start out. If you cannot find any natural learners locally, then work out who is supportive within your community or family of the choice you have made, and nurture those relationships. When people discover what you are doing, you will encounter many positive responses. Librarians, neighbours, old friends and new friends may become mentors, advocates and champions of your family. I have personally spoken to several school principals who have applauded what we were doing. I've also encountered many teachers who understood how rich a life without school can be. Vibrant online communities offer a never-ending stream of help, advice and connection. However, the in-person connection with like-minded families is invaluable.

COMMUNITIES OF NATURAL LEARNERS

We are blessed to have an extensive network of natural learners in Aotearoa New Zealand. We now have several national retreats or camps a year, and these are life-affirming events that provide an escape from the world of constant questions. The value and importance of gathering with like-minded people cannot be underestimated. Hundreds of natural learners meet at camps throughout the year where connection and joy are cultivated through spending time together – at the beach, in hot pools, camping or surfing. We have markets, concerts, workshops, sporting activities, dances, discussions, support networks, shared meals, women's and men's circles, campfires and specific celebrations. Recently we acknowledged a family with seven children whose youngest is now 18 years old. At our summer retreat we organised an afternoon for this dedicated mother to come together with six of her grown children and they shared their story spanning more than 30 years. The celebration was an inspiration to us all, triggering many tears, memories and reflections of the children's own journeys. We sang songs, gave gifts and celebrated with a cake. This was as close to a graduation ceremony as we have ever had, and a new tradition was possibly born out of this close community celebration.

INSECURITIES AND EXPECTATIONS

You may need to let go of the preconceived ideas you have carried over from your own school days or upbringing. Some people may criticise you. Criticism generally comes from a place of fear, which is understandable when you are going against the norm. Perhaps your family are teachers, or value formal education highly, and they may oppose your decision to become natural learners.

You or your partner may have loved school and did well there, so see no reason why your children should not follow the same educational path – after all, everyone else goes to school. It is what we do in our society, so why should your children miss out on what the majority are doing? Or perhaps school was a nightmare for you, and you have a sense that you failed academically and socially and now feel ill-equipped to educate your own children. You may have a residual sense of fear or be in awe of schools and the authority they demand. I have, for instance, spoken with parents who were fearful of going to a school meeting with a principal, because it triggered strong negative memories from their own school days.

Such fears are all real and extremely common and are often felt by at least one parent. I have been asked many times to speak to a partner to try to convince them that natural learning will 'work' for their child. All I can do in these situations is share my own story and offer my experience of natural learning as an inspiration to them. Often one parent is unsure about the teenage years, so they enjoy talking to teenagers who are natural learners and seeing how well-balanced, happy and sociable they are. Fathers who have doubts have often been encouraged to meet with other fathers from families of natural learners to express their concerns and hopefully receive support and reassurance.

You may find you need to rethink how you define education if you are comparing natural learning to traditional schooling. You may believe education is only found in classrooms with books and testing and a qualified teacher at the helm. A mental shift must occur for you to let go of these set ideas and to actively stop comparing what your children are doing with what those attending school are doing. It is like trying to compare chalk and cheese – pointless.

RESOURCING

Parents engaged with natural learning education have a huge role to play in resourcing their children's play and providing for the needs of their children. With young children you may find yourself running around finding things they ask for. Deciding to educate your offspring at home does not mean that you need to purchase expensive items that are deemed to be educational. Children are endlessly creative, and in many ways the less you have the easier it is for them to create a game. Toys that provide open-ended possibilities are the best thing to have; the basics of water, sand/soil, sticks or blocks and basic art supplies will inspire creativity like nothing else. Whatever you have easy access to will be enough to provide them with the learning they seek.

In a world driven by consumerism, we can easily

fall into the trap of believing we need to acquire more possessions, and that buying objects and gadgets will make our lives better. Parents are easy targets of advertising campaigns because they naturally want the best for their children. As a parent you may find well-meaning relatives buy your child toys that engage them for only a short time and offer little educational value or opportunity for creative play. Children do not need expensive, manufactured items to learn about the world. Toys that only allow one way to play can block a child's creativity, so choose carefully what you bring into your home. You can ask relatives and friends to buy only wooden toys, consumable art supplies, experiences or books as gifts.

Another approach is to talk to your children about consumerism, over-packaging, sweatshops and the crippling inequality that exists in the world. In this way you can encourage them to re-gift the excess toys they have. Children are usually understanding and open to helping others who are less privileged. This exercise can be a wonderful way to experience giving, kindness, showing empathy and simplifying life. Gifting money or your time to charities also provides a rich learning experience of real life and a time of bonding as a family. I know families that spend Christmas day serving food to homeless people and they all love it. This takes the emphasis completely off acquiring possessions, while giving your children the valuable experience of service to others.

Spending money on experiences is one way to stop the flow of possessions into your lives. Shared experiences are rich with learning and serve to strengthen family bonds as you create memories together. If you can afford it, then attending festivals, workshops, concerts or courses together, or paying for holidays or adventure activities can be more educational and formative than any toy. Having a family subscription to a magazine or membership to a club can open new doors for even more adventures and hands-on learning.

> **THE STUFF WE HAD**
>
> I did get excited when we started natural learning. The teacher in me purchased some 'educational' items – a globe, magnets, electrical circuit basics and art supplies. It soon became clear that the kids valued anything they could create themselves from whatever they could find, so it was original and perfectly fitted their purpose. Driftwood, cardboard packaging, shells, stones, everyday items like buckets, towels, cutlery, or a broom were constantly repurposed for games.
>
> We certainly accumulated plenty of stuff over the years. We would go to our annual library sale and end up with a huge collection of books on every topic imaginable. We'd also acquire quality board games, more books for Christmas presents, a trampoline, a kayak, bikes, balls, scooters – all the usual trappings of growing up in a privileged Kiwi home. However, I would let the kids themselves instigate what they wanted and was always happy to help find the things they needed for a game or project. Some of the most imaginative games have been played with a simple stick or two.

An easy trap to fall into as a parent is having expectations around what your child will do with the resources you have presented. I remember setting up paints one day and imagining the kids all wanting to paint, producing pictures for the walls. They weren't interested. All day the paints sat there, until finally Charlie, the youngest, started to do some mixing. He had a wonderful time mixing the paints into a brownish-grey brew, but he never had any intention of painting.

PLAYING WITH THE ELEMENTS

Nature provides more than enough for our children to play with while grounding them and letting them see what shapes our world. Water, earth or sand, air and fire all provide a calming and creative play arena. If we were at a beach, lake or river, the kids would drift happily away for a whole day, quickly getting into a game that involved a lot of creativity and construction – a dam, a base, a hut, a village.

Fire is fascinating, soothing and cheap. Learning to collect tinder, to light and sustain a fire and to cook on it is a skill that is seldom taught today, but is an essential survival skill and one that can give a child a sense of satisfaction, connection and self-worth. Having an outdoor fire pit was important for me, and when the kids built a hut nearby, a village atmosphere was created, with lunch being cooked on the fire and kids pottering around or whittling. A good inside fire-based activity that saw my kids well engaged was melting candles and crayons. With old metal trays from the op shop, lots of wax crayons and old candles they would be content and focused for hours.

Time is the most valuable resource we have. Giving your children the opportunity to be at home and the space to play is enough. Do not think you must have money to buy equipment or toys when you need them. There are many places available in our communities where toys, books, tools and instruments can be borrowed or hired. The world is flooded with second-hand and perfectly reusable objects that people are only too happy to pass on when asked. Acquiring the resources your children require or ask for does not need to be an added expense to your lives. Use your creativity and ask for help when needed.

SAYING 'YES' TO YOUR CHILDREN

Saying 'yes' to your children is an important parenting practice that is affirming and empowering for a child. It lets your child know that you are listening to them. You confirm that you believe in them and in their power to create the life they want. You are telling them with a whole-hearted belief that they can have whatever they want. It may not be today, it may be different to what they imagined, it may never actually eventuate, but saying 'yes' is a way of supporting them with your true intention that you will help them reach their heart's desire.

Saying 'yes' to a child can also lessen or remove the dynamic of a powerful adult trying to control them. A child will feel disempowered when their path to success or happiness is blocked by a parent who isn't affirming. A controlling adult will turn a light off in a child's eyes quicker than anything, especially when it is a common occurrence. The anger and frustration a child may feel when their ideas or wishes are routinely blocked, curbed or controlled can be bottled up and compounded over time. In turn this may lead to emotional explosions, to secrecy or telling lies as they are forced to suppress their feelings, and worst of all may result in a loss of belief in themselves. The dampening of enthusiasm, energy, excitement, passion and the desire to question and learn is a terrible thing for anybody. In a child the extinguishing of the creative spark can be soul-destroying.

Saying 'yes' to your child may be the start of a process of stepping towards their end goal. For example, their question, 'Can I learn to play the piano?' may result in listening to some piano music, visiting somewhere they can play on a piano, advertising for someone who wants to give away an instrument, or finding a teacher and a place to practise.

A young child who says, 'I want to go to space,' may have a short-lived childhood dream based on fantasy. But it may result in a period when they are engaged in space-related play, reading and questions. It may mean trips to an observatory and nights out stargazing. If your child expresses interest in space as a teenager, you could support them by looking at formal qualifications and how best to help them move in the right direction – looking up the NASA website, listening to interviews with astronauts, or helping them enrol in physics and maths classes. The outcome of these activities is unimportant – whether the child becomes a musician or an astronaut is not the point. They may well end up in these professions, but the process of saying 'yes' and supporting them for as long as they are motivated and interested is where the meaningful learning happens.

Saying 'yes' to your children means they have rich lives full of a variety of experiences. It also ensures they are empowered to believe they can have the lives they want, something that will have a significant effect on them as they grow up. Many adults don't believe in themselves enough to go and get what they really want in life. Many of us are riddled with doubts and fears, such as:

'Will I be good enough?'
'What if I fail?'
'What will others think?'
'I will never make it, so there's no point in trying.'
'I am too old/not qualified enough.'
'I can't sing/paint/dance/play rugby.'

The confidence that is gained by children who know they have creative licence is a wild and wonderful thing to witness. Once the kids realise the boundaries, understand the family culture and know they will be loved, no matter what, they can relax and let their creative selves dream big.

SELF-DIRECTED CONFIDENCE

I remember on one occasion seeing the kids packing up lunch boxes of food one evening when they were all under 10 years of age. They told me in an offhand way that they were having a midnight feast, and I then proved useful as I could suggest possible food items. They were not being at all secretive. It had just not occurred to them to tell me what they were planning as I wasn't invited, so the midnight feast didn't affect me.

Another time I found them heaving mattresses onto a flat piece of roof on our house, which they regularly climbed on to play. They had decided they would sleep up there for the night along with some friends who were visiting. I was never part of the equation. I heard them talking about safety concerns and problem-solving issues that could arise, while their determination drove them on to realise their idea of sleeping outdoors on the roof. I love that they had the confidence to know I would say 'yes' if asked, but they had not thought there was a need to gain permission.

I have always tried to say 'yes' to pretty much everything my children have asked. This may seem ludicrous to some parents, but it has been the route to a peaceful and fulfilled (not to mention colourful and creative) life for all concerned.

> **QUESTIONS THAT I HAVE BEEN SAYING 'YES' TO FOR YEARS**
> - Can I eat my dinner floating on a tray in the bath/in our hut/in the park?
> - Can we keep the whole lounge set up as a shop? (For months and months)
> - Can I go out naked in the snow?
> - Can I wear my (favourite, ripped) tutu and gumboots to the wedding?
> - Can we stay at the beach until it is dark? (That is, until the end of the day when everyone else has left, and I have three exhausted kids and an hour's drive home.)
> - Can my friend stay the night, again? (Third night in a row.)

> - Can you read this book again?
> - Can I cook dinner?
> - Can I go to drama class/play the horn/join cadets?

Often children just want to know they are allowed to do what they ask. It doesn't mean they will actually do it. For instance, when one of my children was eight years old they asked if they could try breastfeeding again. I said 'yes', but they just shrugged and said, 'Okay, good', and didn't pursue it. We all want the opportunity to make our own choices. Children creating the learning for themselves is at the heart of natural learning. No matter how sure you are of the outcome, or how badly you want to do it for them to keep things tidy, quick, or done 'properly', the best, deepest, and most long-lasting learning comes from the child's personal experience.

Parenting in this child-empowering way gave my kids a building block of courage from which to live the life they eventually chose – what they wanted, not what I wanted for them. Parents wish their kids to be happy, but many young people are weighed down by parental expectations of what they consider to be achievement and success. As adults it is easy to believe we know what is best for our child – it's an easy trap to fall into. There are times that we do know best – safety issues are non-negotiable, for instance. Other times I have tried to listen attentively to what my child is expressing, then checked to see if it was my ego answering or my heart accepting another's needs.

The biggest learning around this has been taught to me by my children who have often said to me, 'If you want to be an artist/doctor/builder (fill in whatever you imagine would be best for your kids) then you do it. I am not interested.' I may think I know what is best for my children but this does not mean I am right. They themselves know best. This is good advice that I try to stick to.

SAYING 'YES' TO ASPIRATIONS

At the age of 12 Ollie came home from Scouts one day telling me the World Scout Jamboree would be held in Japan in two years' time, at a cost of $6000. Ollie had been to the national Jamboree the previous year and it had been the best experience of his life so far. He was buzzing for months afterwards. I didn't need to ask him if he wanted to go to Japan. Seeing the hope and the belief in his face and hearing the pure excitement was all I needed. 'Sign up,' I said. 'Tell them you are going, and we will get you there.' That affirmation marked the beginning of 18 months of fundraising. At times we both needed to draw on different skills to motivate Ollie and keep the dream of attending the Jamboree alive for him. But neither he nor I ever wavered in our belief that he would go. Of course, he went and had another formative and wonderful time. He was also extremely grateful for all the support I gave him and appreciated the work that got him there. But it all stemmed from saying 'yes' at the outset.

PLAY IS A CHILD'S WORK

Playing is how children learn about the world. An adult is best occupied by listening to the kids, watching them, maybe recording what is happening in their play, then finding resources when the kids ask for them. If they ask you, the adult, to play along with them, let them take the lead and go along with their mandate. Children are clear about what their game is, so all you have to do is follow instructions – 'Lie down and sleep for 100 years until I gallop up and kiss you,' or 'You be this digger, drive it to the farm,' or 'Pretend you are the patient with a broken leg, and I will be the doctor.' Do not get involved if you are not invited to or try to control a child's play so they do it 'properly'. Their own way is the proper way, the exact and perfect way for them at that time.

By being aware of the game there is less chance you will insist they stop it, pack it up or change it to suit your own needs. Let them follow through with their play and be who they are. A child's creative force is strong. They can host a picnic for 20 teddies and be happy with imaginary tea and food. They are masterful creators and inventors. Need a telescope or a control panel? Instantly someone invents one. What about boats for 50 plastic animals? Within seconds they find a solution and the game goes on, the players undeterred by the makeshift 'boats', not seeing them as books all over the floor, and staying fully focused on the 50 creatures adrift on the ocean. If adults were aware of or were joining in the game, they would have an understanding of what the books all over the floor represented and why the furniture was placed the way it was. An uninvolved adult could easily misunderstand the depth of the game and see only a mess, which they then would clear up to satisfy their own needs for tidiness, ignoring the needs of the playing child and effectively destroying the game.

FOLLOWING A MAGICAL PATH

As the children grew, their imaginations grew with them, and games became increasingly complex. When Hannah was 11 years old, she and her friends set up 'St Hedwigs Collegiate School for Girls' a Harry Potter-inspired school, which each of the three families involved took turns hosting for them. I was given a lot of instruction and guidance about what was expected of me in my role as teacher. Hannah and I planned the lessons together in the days before we were hosting the school. This entailed me asking questions and Hannah telling me where I could have creative license (my knowledge of the world was reasonably good) and when I was to follow her detailed lesson plan. I dressed up and 'taught' the lessons I was asked to. Thoughtfully, Hannah had tried to incorporate areas I enjoyed: Herbology where we could wander around the garden picking leaves to stick in their books with descriptions; music, where they wrote the school song; history in which each student got to construct their own version of the school's origins. The three friends had op-shopped for matching uniforms and between the three households covered a wide range of subjects.

Children have a never-ending source of original ideas and can clearly think outside the square, especially when uninhibited by an adult's preconceived expectations or social constraints. If you watch closely children are always learning something, exploring and pushing themselves to discover the next thing. The imaginative genius of children consistently astounds me. A child can take a game or a concept and twist it creatively in a way an adult could never have dreamed of. A child can see a rocket, a pirate ship, a raft or a cave where you see only your lounge furniture and a rug or two. Their creative spirit is something to be nurtured and treasured.

I have noticed that my children learn the most when I have respectfully stayed away from their games and left them to it. As Maria Montessori said, 'The great benefit we [adults] can bestow on childhood is the exercise of restraint in ourselves.' Her educational model is famously based on children's play. Unhindered by an idea of what formal learning should look like, my children found the fun in the everyday, and plenty of learning.

STAND BACK AND WATCH THE LEARNING UNFOLD

One day I bought some kitchen scales, retro ones, with a large bowl on the top. We had never had any because I rarely measure things when cooking. The next morning both the boys – then aged four and six – discovered the scales. They unpacked them and instantly started to play with them. As I listened, I was amazed to hear what they were saying and playing. It was straight out of a maths lesson, and I know if I had tried to facilitate such a 'lesson' it would have been a disaster.

They started bringing tins and packets of food out of the cupboard and this is what I heard.

'Let's make it up to 1 kg – how much more do we need?'

'Get a tin of tomatoes, they are 400 grams and then we need another 150.'

'How much does this weigh then?'

'Do you think this will be more than that?'

The quality of the questions, their excitement and their in-the-moment sense of fun was tremendous.

The two boys played for two hours, in their pyjamas, fully engrossed and passionate about their activity. They completed a full unit on measurement by any teacher's standard. Done and dusted, all before breakfast.

There was no need to continue to do this, their learning was complete. There was no need to assess them. Although over the years they would, of course, weigh things again, they never repeated that intensity of discovery they had that morning – they didn't need to.

After more than 20 years of intense parenting I remain convinced that childhood, up to puberty, should, ideally, be spent in play. Never underestimate the power of imagination. Einstein understood its far-reaching potential: 'Imagination is more important than knowledge. For knowledge is limited to all we know and understand, while imagination embraces the entire world, and all there ever will be to know and understand.'

Chapter 6

COMPARISONS AND UNHELPFUL QUESTIONS

When you step out of the mainstream educational system to parent natural learners from home you will inevitably be subjected to questions and judgements from others. Family members and complete strangers will feel they have a right to question why your children are not at school. No matter how enthusiastic a champion of natural learning you may be, responding to these sorts of comments can be tiring. You may become bored having to explain your lifestyle and philosophy to people who don't understand it. You will do well to develop a thick skin and let other people's judgements flow over your head, just as celebrities do.

Everyone who educates their children at home has to deal with the constant refrain of 'No school today?' or 'Having a day off school?' when they are out in the world during school hours. The more we are out and about and interacting with others in the community the more normalised the natural learning lifestyle becomes. However, you will need to decide whether to respond seriously to these sorts of comments and explain your natural learning choice, or whether you simply nod and 'agree'. Being an ambassador for natural learning can feel relentless, and sometimes you simply want to buy a loaf of bread without having to explain or defend your parenting choices. Not offering an explanation or engaging in discussion may be a wise choice in some circumstances and a way of protecting your emotional wellbeing.

HOW DO YOU SOCIALISE?
Socialising is a hot topic for people looking in from the outside to those who educate at home, they often imagine we sit at home all day with the kids working at the kitchen table. The concern about social interaction comes with the assumption that school is the natural way to socialise. I have often countered comments and questions about socialising by saying that I don't believe being in a room all day with 29 of your peers is a natural way to socialise. I offer the insight that I certainly would not want to spend my day with 29 adults the same age as me, as I prefer to choose friends with similar interests or values, not because of our shared age. I would also get exhausted spending each day with so many other people. It would be like attending a party all day, every day.

If people are genuinely interested in how the children socialise, then it may help to list the activities you do as a family, which are often rich in quality time, shared experiences and fun community events, but without the stressful time restraints of having to get to bed or be up early because of school. Children, like adults, enjoy a variety of social interactions. Many people like quiet, intense one-on-one time and may need to recharge after social gatherings. Other people have wide social circles and are out socialising at every opportunity. Living in a natural learning environment helps a child get to know who they are and what fills them up. When practising natural learning we are able to design our lives around our own daily rhythms, which means we have the luxury of being able to socialise as much or as little as we want to.

> **SOCIALISING AT YOUR OWN PACE**
>
> Since leaving home and reflecting back on her natural learning childhood, Hannah has told us that even though she was an introvert and spent a lot of time alone, she enjoyed having so many visitors to our home, when she could come out and interact as much as she wanted and then go back to her own space. Our lifestyle meant we could enjoy full, long weekends away, at festivals and camps with late nights around a fire, big games and swimming. Then come Monday or Tuesday each child could play quietly in their own worlds while recouping and resting. These post-event pyjama days seem to be commonplace among our community of natural learners, reflecting the need that many of us have to recharge.

When you are not following a curriculum or a timetable as natural learners, questions about your educational choices can be harder to answer. Often people get excited to hear what you are doing and ask more questions. However, even the most well-meaning person, like a friendly librarian, can end up making unhelpful comments or asking confusing questions. When my kids were young and were asked 'What are you studying today?' they would not understand the question and would look unsure. I would mentally scrabble around trying to think of something translatable to rescue us all from a full explanation. Occasionally I would feed them ideas for responding in these situations. For instance, if we had been talking about a topic or if there was a strong theme in their play, I would suggest they have their response on hand: 'Today we have been looking at human rights in China,' or 'Lots of cooking this morning.' The concept of natural learning is a challenging one to understand for some people, and it can be difficult to explain in a brief conversation with a stranger. Although I advocate living with integrity and truth at all times if possible, in circumstances like these I would make an exception.

If you have the time, the inclination and the energy, then explaining natural learning to the inquiring person can lead to an engaging conversation. It may turn out to be exactly what the other person needed, and your lifestyle has become an inspiration for them. There have been times when my advocacy for what we do has bordered on the evangelical, for instance when encouraged by an interested parent in a supermarket aisle. I found that explaining only when I felt I had the time and the other person was genuinely interested provided some balance for me.

Sometimes the interaction with others outside the natural learning environment is not so positively engaging. You may be subjected to comments about how you are depriving your children and how they are missing out on an education. Do you defend and debate the issue, or smile and walk away? Humour can sometimes be effective in these situations, but can just as easily backfire with the wrong person. For instance, joking about how your eight-year-old has practically lived in the sand pit or played with Lego for the last four years and so must have a great future as an engineer can be taken the wrong way with the uninitiated. You may choose to counter negative comments with a few examples of the varied learning experiences your children have through their activities – like the business skills they learn from setting up a lemonade or fruit stall, the fund-raising skills they learn from busking, or the maths skills they learn from cooking. Uninterrupted time on a project is hard to achieve in a traditional schooling environment, but in a natural learning setting a child can, for example, spend three consecutive and uninterrupted days working on creating a book for a younger sibling. These examples are easy for others to relate to and provide insights into the value of natural learning.

HOW DO YOU KNOW THEY HAVE LEARNED ANYTHING?

This is a great question. On the one hand when you are with your children all day, every day, and have developed good listening skills, it is amazing what you pick up about their learning. Rather than the adult constantly monitoring and measuring the learning, the children themselves will communicate their progress. They want to share things they have read, made, or are thinking about. Their knowledge will impress you (and others) quite enough when they can reel off informative facts, present an amazing project, or relate a complex game they have set up. The 'proof' (if proof is needed) will be in the pudding, as they say.

On the other hand, it is really none of anyone else's business what your children are learning. I did not judge or measure my children's progress – that was their concern. Besides, who am I to judge whether another person should or should not know something? I believe that, even as their parent, I was not privy to my children's inner lives, nor did I need to know where they were on any continuum of learning. My only job was to support them. I personally am interested in a huge range of topics and people. I love to ask questions, and hear stories, to research and read, but this does not mean I retain everything or want to produce an essay on any of it. Does this mean I haven't learned anything?

Some adults are unsettled by the prospect of natural learning and ask, with horror, how your children will ever be able to operate in the 'real world'. This is one question I feel is important to answer candidly. I don't see school as a reflection of our real existence as an adult, yet it is held up as the best place to learn the skills required for life. I respond to this question by explaining how we are already living fully in the real world, the world that the children are growing up and operating in every day. This is the world where the kids are a part of regular shopping, banking and household management jobs, and where they have adult mentors and friends. By organising themselves and their own daily rhythms, they know themselves extremely well and are learning real life skills of self-management, communication and problem-solving. Natural learners are generally fully engaged members of the 'real world' from a young age. There will not be a transition from a schooling institution to 'real life', just a gentle morphing as they grow.

You will experience times when you feel as though you are being judged and that your children are being checked out or assessed in a way that school-attending children are not. To me this sort of judgement seems grossly unfair as these people do not test school-going children or monitor their academic progress in the same way. The 2016 film 'Captain Fantastic' refreshingly shows the clear advantages of educating children at home. When they test the school-going cousins against the intelligent, free and wild youngsters who have been learning from home, every natural learner is surely cheering them on. It is an unusual treat to see this theme dealt with in a mainstream film.

If you feel it is worthwhile debating the benefits of natural learning to critics or proving to them how well your child is doing and how much better off they are not being in school, then I applaud you. Bullying statistics can provide good fuel for your argument, as can inspirational examples of famous entrepreneurs who 'dropped out' of school. You will help shed an alternative light on school for those who have never considered that another option could be preferential.

AREN'T YOU STOPPING YOUR KIDS FROM EXPERIENCING WHAT OTHER KIDS THEIR AGE EXPERIENCE?

Mostly of course the answer is yes and that is often the point of not going to school. I am happy for my kids not to have experienced what a lot of other children have at school. They did not spend time having to line up, wait for others to finish or settle down, keep changing their focus, or follow someone else's idea of what they should be learning. They may have missed out on being bullied, being bored, or being misunderstood. What they have not missed out on is large tracts of their childhood being spent in ways they would not choose. We have had plenty of time for all the good stuff and without a doubt, our children have been lucky to experience a far richer life than many of their peers in school.

Children will find their own way to respond to curious adults wanting to know more about what they do all day. Many children educated at home are happy to share about their lives, often with total honesty and openness. A confident or outgoing child may delight in explaining their lives to strangers or adult friends. Quieter or shy children may find such interest uncomfortable so having conversations about this ahead of time can help prepare them.

Having some stock answers could help them too. For the question 'no school today?' A child may want to explain the basics - 'I am educated at home', 'I don't go to school', 'my parents teach me' or 'we homeschool'. For the next level of inquiry about 'what are you studying?' Some generic answers may be a good start - 'lots of things', 'all my favourite things', 'I like playing _____', 'we are going shopping/swimming' or 'today I have been at the park/beach.'

Whether you view the questions or concerns of others as a chance to engage in a conversation or an annoyance, learning to deal with them gracefully is another skill to be acquired. There are more and more people interested in education at home and having an increasing number of us out there and talking about our lives is, hopefully, mostly inspiring to others.

Chapter 7

READING, WRITING AND MATHS

Reading, writing and maths are regarded as the foundation of a regular education and form the cornerstone of the school curriculum. So how does a child who is allowed to do what they want ever learn these skills? You may be surprised and possibly challenged to think there is an alternative way to learn the basics without specific tuition or resources.

Much of the required curriculum that has been chosen for those at school is not difficult and for many students much of it is not relevant in my view. Adults who attended school themselves may be apprehensive about letting go of the familiar ways they were taught traditional school subjects. You may need to let go of any expectations around education while supporting your young ones on their self-directed approach to learning reading, writing and maths. Your own bias and experiences from school will be at the fore. More than ever, this is a time to let go of your beliefs and trust the process that will unfold.

Imagine a system where students get to choose what they specialise in at every level of their education – musicians, artists, builders, engineers, writers, designers, cooks, gardeners, scientists and athletes all being able to dedicate time to their passions as young children and teenagers. With no leaning towards any particular subjects, their confidence would build easily while they were young learners, and they would be empowered to believe in themselves. As they develop, their learning could naturally dovetail into further study or work that is relevant to their skills and interests. This is the reality for many natural learners.

LEARNING TO READ

How will your kids ever learn to read? After all, in school the teachers have training based on years of research and practice, and a programme that is proven to work, with special books and specific follow-up work. In a school, children are tested regularly, then allocated a reading age. If this is under the expected norm, then a remedial programme is introduced. When a child is left to do what they want, how does reading ever happen?

Reading is a highly valued skill to have, representative of having an education. Because of the importance reading is seen to have, a parent who is naturally supporting a child to read can feel it is an area laden with responsibility. Learning to read has more focus placed on it than other skills, perhaps placing stress and expectations around the process that a child may pick up. Although young children often memorise texts to please adults, there is no ambiguity around whether a person can read or not. This can also mean parents are motivated to have their child read as early as possible, so they feel successful as a home-educating parent.

When you remove a child from this structured environment and let them play, their journey towards learning to read may look vastly different. With no testing or expectations, the joy of reading should be modelled and supported by you, as this will be the foundation of your child's reading. Reading becomes just another skill to be acquired, like walking or riding a bike. Reading becomes a way to decode what they see and a means of gaining information from the world of words and text. A young child is decoding all they see around them, making sense of the world of words, be it books, magazines, signs, notes, posters or letters. Give children a text-rich environment and curiosity will prevail. Let them see you reading, and they too will want 'in' on this sought-after skill.

The last couple of decades have seen huge changes in the types of text we are reading. In a high-tech age, where phones and computers are part of everyday life for most of us, what we absorb and read every day is most likely to be on a screen. We are still to find out what the consequences of this might be, but be assured if your child is surrounded only by computers, television, PlayStation, iPads, phones or other devices, then you need not expect them to sit down and read a book. They will still be reading text and learning from what they see, but on a screen instead and for the purpose of learning to read this may make little difference. If books and magazines are not part of your family culture, or don't play an important role in their lives they can still learn to read from the content they are mostly spending time with online. Perhaps they will not become book readers, but you can expect your children to become experts at navigating a laptop, a whizz using the apps on your phone or computer and touch typists.

> **READING IS LIKE BREATHING**
>
> It would have been near impossible for a child to have grown up in our house without reading. For years I read to the kids constantly. We had books everywhere and they saw us adults reading. Visiting the library was a common activity when the kids were young, when they would check out the maximum of 20 books each at least once a week. We had no television, which, although extremely unusual in our society, is common in the natural learning circles we move in. I was more than happy to have a screen-free environment for the kids to spend their early years in, although I understand how this is getting harder every year as technology prevails in most walks of life.

Reading will happen naturally when a child is ready if you provide a rich, text-positive environment, follow their lead, and support their interests. Learning to read naturally from books will happen if you engage regularly in at least some of the following.

- Read to your child often, continuing into their teenage years if possible.
- Have lots of books in the house and value them.
- Go on regular trips to the library where they can choose their own books.
- Make time to read and explore the books they

are interested in, re-reading, pointing things out and answering questions.
- Have adults and siblings around them who read.
- Suggest family and friends give books as birthday gifts.
- Share the text you see around you – signs, letters, fridge magnets, name badges.

Learning to read may not happen at five or six years of age, as is expected at school. It may also happen suddenly, especially if the child is older. Be assured that if your child is eight, nine or 10 years old and still not keen to read, it will happen. There are plenty of examples of late readers in our natural learning community. If you are worried, find some parents you can talk to, keep reading to your children, and relax.

LEARNING TO READ AGES VARY

One friend had a daughter who was not reading at all at the age of 10. When she was 11, she suddenly started reading and could read well almost overnight. The following year she went to school and when her reading age was tested, it was well over 14 years – with just two years of reading.

At the other end of the spectrum Hannah taught herself to read purely through asking questions the year she was four – 'What does that sign say?', 'How do you spell . . . ?' I was pregnant through all this time with Charlie and when he was born, Hannah could already read competently, and she was reading the Harry Potter books to herself before she was six.

These examples above show that learning to read can be a natural process and does not need to be forced. A child coerced into reading may not become a lifelong reader. Reading should be a joy that is modelled, encouraged and supported – like any other interest.

Reading to my children (and I have clocked up some serious mileage here) was one of my greatest parenting pleasures. It meant we were all excited to get into bed at night. It meant a relaxing shared activity of pure escapism and fantasy that sometimes would fill in most of a day – lying in a park or snuggled up by the fire in winter. It meant upon returning from town with their stash of library books it was perfectly normal for the kids to stay in the car reading while I unpacked the groceries and cooked dinner. They would often head inside only when it was too dark to read or if they had finished all their books. Their Dad would get home two hours after we had and ask where one of the children was, only to find they were still out in the car, absorbed in a whole different world.

HOW CHARLIE LEARNED TO READ

Charlie was six years old when the children in our family went through the Asterix phase. Although I usually said 'yes' to requests to read to my children, reading Asterix was one of the few exceptions – I just found graphic books too fiddly. When Charlie asked me to read them to him, wanting to copy his older siblings, I explained that I really didn't want to. He would still 'read' them to himself, keeping up with the others. After several months I noticed that his lips were moving when reading them. I asked him if he could read, and he said he could. I then asked if he would read me a picture book, which he was happy to do and did with ease. I would never have picked comics as a learn-to-read text, but his motivation was strong, and his pathway was happily paved with the fantastical tales of Obelix and Dogmatrix.

Some people, children included, find non-fiction is often more interesting than fiction, as it helps facilitate their interests. A non-fiction book, a graphic comic, magazines, newspapers, letters, notes from you – any text is reading, and all are valuable. I would encourage parents to let children choose their own reading material and to help them learn to use the library system. Librarians love to be asked questions, and it is heart-warming to see your young child asking for help to find a book on a topic they love. It is a wonderful chance for both the child and the librarian to build a relationship and for your child to practise operating in the 'real world' while also helping to raise the profile of natural learners in the community.

If a child is actively learning to read, with their finger following each letter or each word, how and when should you help? Is this a valuable learning opportunity or should you just leave them to it? It depends on the context and the personality of the child. You want to encourage them without making them feel stupid, powerless or like giving up. Imagine, for instance, a child is busy and focused on playing a game and needs to read something to gain an instant understanding, so they call out for help. It is clear they need the information quickly and are not after a reading lesson.

When a young reader is pointing to letters and words trying to make sense of the text, this is still a perfectly natural learning situation that does not need your intervention. If you feel they are getting frustrated, you could ask them if they want your help and to clarify how much help they want. They may want to know only the sound of one letter, or one word. Those kids who are persistent and confident with the learning process feel perfectly fine working things out in their own way, yet we may interpret this as struggling. Try not to project your own feelings onto a situation. Think of the baby learning to walk, falling over continuously and yet getting up time and again to keep on trying. How did you respond to this? Apply this to a child starting to read and realise that for them reading may not be frustrating or hard, it is just another new thing to master, a new set of skills to claim.

Consider learning to read as being similar to learning to walk or talk. If children are supported to learn in their own time and style and have none of your fears or expectations put onto them it will be a joyous time of discovery – quite different from an enforced reading lesson.

MATHS IS A NATURAL PART OF EVERYDAY LIFE

Maths is everywhere. For young children, maths learning occurs naturally through their play. Maths is part of any game or activity where counting, measuring, or ordering is needed. Activities like cooking, creating artwork or models offer chances to learn and practise maths skills. Playing with older siblings or friends boosts the learning, which can happen quickly and without you even realising. Maths concepts are learned by children through their wondering and being curious about things around them, by talking to the adults in their lives, taking risks and feeling safe to do so. Like all learning, maths concepts are much richer when made while playing or creating, and the lesson sticks more easily when it happens in a real-life context.

However, maths learning can cause a large amount of stress for parents of natural learners. Many adults have negative memories of learning maths at school, often telling themselves they are no good at maths, that they don't like maths, or that they are stupid. Adults often hold onto the notion that there is only one way to solve a maths problem, whereas modern maths is very different to how maths used to be taught. Some parents may feel inadequate to be their child's maths teacher in any way. The fear of not having maths knowledge often leads natural learning parents to use a textbook with their children and do regular classroom-style, book learning maths lessons. This approach may be the one exception to the child-led, play-based way the child may be learning the rest of the time. The adult's fear is real and comes from a heavily biased education system, where they were made to believe that we will need the maths that is taught in schools to function in everyday life.

For years I have been collecting anecdotal data about the usefulness of the maths adults learned at school by asking them how much of the maths they learned at high school they have used in their adult lives. More often than I imagined they are like me and say none, unless they are accountants, engineers, builders, scientists, teachers or working in similar fields. Complex maths of the sort that is taught in high school is often not required by many in their everyday life. Maths knowledge and the associated skills are a vital part of everyday life, used by most people to some degree, but not to the extent I was led to believe as a teenager. The maths I use to organise my life is more basic – and it is what my children learned during their young lives:

> **WHAT CONSTITUTES EVERYDAY MATHS FOR ME**
> - Telling the time – analogue and digital, using a stopwatch, calculating time.
> - Mental addition – grocery shopping, working out pocket money, scoring in games and household budgeting.
> - Estimating distance and spatial awareness – throwing a ball, shooting an arrow, cycling, driving.
> - Measuring (weight, distance, volume, etc) – cooking, creating and building 3-D objects, reading maps
> - Percentages, fractions and ratios – cooking, craft/building projects, shopping, sharing.

It took me years to realise that I have never used all the maths that I sweated over in high school. I have a degree, own a house, have raised children, play music, teach, write, garden, stay healthy, negotiate relationships and travel – all without needing to use cosine, square root, algebra or trigonometry. It is true for me the maths I had to study at 15 and 16 years of age was a stressful experience that left me feeling I was no good at the subject. I wonder how different I would have been if my education was one where I could have learned the exact amount of maths I needed at a young age and with relative ease in a real-life setting? This would have left me time and energy to stay focused on the subjects that I loved.

My experience is that much of the maths I was taught in high school was never used again and was therefore a waste of my time and energy. An often repeated saying of mine about the sort of maths that we all use in everyday life is, 'It's not rocket science,' unless it actually is. The fact that there is a chunk of highly technical maths knowledge that has been deemed vital for all of us to learn and be tested on reveals a system weighted towards math knowledge.

> **USE IT OR LOSE IT**
> Hannah asked me about what square root was. She had heard students in her drama class talking about a maths test and felt she was missing out. So I explained it to her. The following year, she asked me again and I explained again. The next year when she asked, we had a laugh, and I pointed out exactly what this showed, that she was not using square root in her life, so right now it was redundant knowledge. Who cared if she forgot it?

Many parents of natural learners want to know what mathematical knowledge young children need. They may wonder how children learn maths while 'just playing'. When we first started natural learning, I did have occasional worries about the children not seeming to be learning or 'doing' any maths. They came to the rescue early on, as they always did, and showed me that maths is everywhere and is fascinating when it is relevant.

> **DINNERTIME MATHS**
>
> I had made filo pastry parcels for dinner and took the first load out to the kids at the table and went to retrieve the second lot. My ego had a nice boost while they discussed how delicious they were. Then I heard the conversation that followed: 'These are good enough for a café', 'So what would you pay for one?', 'How many are you going to have?', 'Ok, well that one is $8, but these ones are smaller so I think they should be $3.50 each. I'll eat three of them, so that's $10.50.' You get the picture. They honestly sounded like a scripted maths lesson! I couldn't believe it. They were doing maths around the dinner table, without a prompt, and completely in earnest. It was real life, relevant and fun. It was just the gift I needed to show that when children are interested in the world around them, they will learn whether you like it or not.

My experience is that young children, up to puberty, will learn what they need through play and will mostly not exceed your knowledge of basic everyday maths concepts – measurement, time, basic arithmetic, times tables and estimation. Their learning is demonstrated in many fascinating and creative ways because, as usual, the children themselves find a way to set up lessons, extend themselves and even test themselves. Two of my kids did some formal maths learning early on at their own behest. At just three years of age Hannah asked for sheets of maths sums that I had written (basic addition and subtraction), and strangely enough she wanted these, with a picnic breakfast, left by her bed so when she woke up she would complete the maths 'work' straight away while eating breakfast.

THE MOST COMMITTED MATHEMATICIAN

Charlie also asked for maths sums, but late at night – at 10pm or later. Coming up with what was essentially a maths worksheet after a full day of parenting was challenging. He was four years old and was asking for equations like 38 + 87. At the age of five, he moved his maths up to the next level and for nearly a whole year he played shops intensively. This meant we were all issued with our own container of play money. Doorways, walls and cupboards were covered in advertisements he had written up letting us know what services he was offering and how much they cost (massage and gambling services among them, which caused some hilarity with visitors). Our lounge and all its contents were priced. By this I mean they had pieces of paper taped to them with complex prices. The sofa was $173.98, the table $549.25, books arranged in neat rows on the floor were $3.76, the pantry contents spent most of the year in the shop, which guaranteed him a customer when I was about to cook dinner and needed ingredients.

We all got a bit sick of it at times, but we all played along. Even visitors were instantly issued with money and encouraged to come shopping. When you bought several items, Charlie added them up accurately in his head in record time and issued

> the correct change. He was constantly challenging himself with the complex prices and the ensuing equations. He was in heaven as a retailer. One highlight was a period of about a month where several other regular (child) visitors were drawn into the game. The whole house now became a thriving marketplace, called 'Market 73.' We had a postal service, a newspaper, a fruit and vege shop, a bank, a wide range of unusual services and advertisements everywhere – I would still find them years later. This was a wonderful game that mimicked real life, and the buzz it created was huge, especially for Charlie who was living his dream and naturally extending his mathematical practice and knowledge.

As children grow and seek more, those who are drawn to numbers may need resources and skills that you don't possess. If you feel inadequate, then reach out – there are plenty of maths resources, books, online games, courses, private and other tuition that are available. Any online forum is full of parents debating the merits of resources, especially around maths knowledge. If your child wants more than what you can give, then of course you ask for help and find new ways to do things. This is no different to a child wanting to learn a musical instrument or take up karate. It is a specialised skill offered by others and applying this approach to academic subjects like maths is a perfectly sensible path to take.

If you find your teenage children are more drawn to arts subjects, that is if the things they are interested in and spend their days absorbed in are language-based, art-based, or creative design work or similar, then they probably know and are already using all the maths concepts they need for now and will learn other concepts as they go, organically.

I am not at all anti-maths. It is everywhere around us and in use constantly as we engage with life. I enjoy using maths in real life contexts and have a quick brain for arithmetic. I am an artist in the sense I write, play music, paint and have an arts degree, yet at the same time I have supported my children to follow their interests – hopefully in the same way as a parent who is not artistic, but supports their children to follow that path if they choose.

Veteran homeschooling mother and maths enthusiast Denise Gaskins states, 'You don't need a set of worksheets or lesson plans to learn math. All you need is an inquiring mind and something interesting to think about. Play. Discuss. Notice. Wonder. Enjoy.' This sounds like a true and accurate definition of natural learning.

LEARNING TO WRITE

There are two distinct aspects of 'writing'. First, there is the practical skill of holding a pen and learning to form letters. Then writing skills evolve to include learning about sentence structure and grammar while writing for a particular purpose.

Because writing is conveyed visually, it is a form of expression that people are quick to judge a child on – and sometimes also their parents. A child with undeveloped handwriting might be considered unintelligent by people who are used to measuring their children's progress according to the school system. Yet writing forms part of play for a child and will develop instinctively as and when needed throughout their childhood.

It is easy to compare your child's handwriting to one at school who practises daily from age five or six. When left to do their own thing, children may not end up doing much writing, if any at all, for years. Within the natural learning community, I have met children who had no interest in writing until they were eight or nine, or even older.

Learning to form letters can be a playful part of everyday life – making pancakes or bread dough into letters, twirling spaghetti into letters, writing in the sand or on dusty cars. You can model this as an adult as a part of everyday life. There is no need for special books or for expectations that your child will want to write anything when you think they should. My personal philosophy has always been to promptly help spell out a word when asked, not to expect a child to 'sound' it out. How frustrating for them when they are in the middle of making a treasure map to stop and perform spelling exercises for an adult who holds all the power. Resourcing and supporting your child in their play is the best you can do.

> **LEARNING TO WRITE AT AGE 10**
>
> When Ollie moved up from Cubs to Scouts at the age of 10, he had to take along a notebook to write weekly notices in. I felt conflicted about what to do as he could barely write. I felt it was a good strategy to forewarn him and describe what was considered 'normal', even though it was hard for me to do. I explained to him that all the other Scouts had been writing every day at school for five years and so their handwriting was more like mine. I said that some of the other 10-year-olds may judge him or make

comments about his writing seeming babyish. I offered to help do some writing at home if he wanted to and suggested he ask the leader how to spell words if needed. He seemed completely unfazed and went off to Scouts. At first, his lack of writing skills was harshly judged by others who thought he must be stupid. But luckily his huge knowledge of all things Scouting quickly gave him status and made him a leader. Others quickly realised he had many skills that they did not – so who cared about his writing?

Once the basic mechanics of handwriting are learned, then writing becomes a tool to express your intention across a range of genres. In the school system children write speeches, poetry, stories, persuasive text, debates, letters, articles and reports. In this system, if your child isn't writing stories about what they did 'on the weekend' by the time they are six years old, society may give you messages that your child is behind, missing out, or not learning all they should be.

Never fear, because just like reading, walking and talking, children learn to write when they need to. With the resources needed to write – pens, paper, chalk etc – support from you, and the inspiration that is found all around them, children will naturally want to be recording, communicating, explaining and creating if the written word is part of the world around them.

Take a moment to think about how often you write. In what circumstances in your life do you need to write? How much writing do you do in your everyday life or in your job? Perhaps, like many of us, the sum of your written language comes down to writing birthday cards, shopping and to-do lists, short reminder notes to others to put the rubbish bins out or feed the chickens, or perhaps you keep a personal journal or write a bit of poetry. In reality, it's probably not much at all – certainly no stories about 'What I did in the holidays'.

Times are changing, and as much as I love the physicality of pen and paper, computers have become a big part of our everyday life. In the last few years computer use in schools has increased to an extent where it is normal for students to use a device all day and writing with a pen on paper has basically become defunct. Touch typing is a good skill to have and one that may develop naturally when you are on a keyboard for long enough. While I grieve the loss of pen and paper, I also embrace the new technology available. We are in a time of transition where kids are competent on a computer, yet young people are finishing their school years unable to write particularly well or '2 rite prpr englsh n e more bt who R gr8 texters'.

With your support, children can easily learn to write naturally as part of their play, especially when they are exposed to plenty of text in a relaxed environment.

WHEN OLLIE WAS 11

This is from a journal note I wrote about Ollie's writing, back when he was 11. 'Ollie has always hated to write, so it was lovely to see him doing it for fun as he got older. He wrote a song this morning, wrote the whole thing out and then performed it at a homeschool event this afternoon too. On holiday he even started writing a journal. He keeps lists in notebooks of survival items and takes notes from survival books that would please any Year 7 teacher trying to teach note taking.'

One of the things that I quickly learned to let go of was to have written 'proof' of my children's learning. There was no need for testing, reports or writing samples. I have never made the kids write down something to prove that they knew it. We shared conversations which showed critical and deep thinking. They did plenty of reading, always asking lots of questions yet never produced written proof they had learned or retained knowledge from the topic. They were in charge of what they needed to learn and knew I would help when needed.

Reading, being reciprocal, is a great and natural stepping stone to acquiring the skill of writing. If you pay attention, you will see that writing comes into early play, so support that unconditionally by not interrupting their play to test them. Model writing for them – leave them notes, write them poems, songs, stories or lists and share whatever you are moved to write. If you keep a record of what they are up to, let them help write it or see what you have written. All this is surrounding them with text in a real-life context.

Children will write when they need to, when it is relevant, and when they are surrounded by text. So let them play, and trust that you will be called upon to spell out the odd word or ten to aid them in their life's work – which is play.

Chapter 8

SCIENCE IN PLAY

Science can be relatively easy for a parent to spot in a child's work: playing with sand and water, sticks and stones, gardening, cooking, making a fire, watching the night sky and investigating or caring for animals will all contain science-based learning. Research is conducted naturally by young inquiring minds as they test out different theories and change the variables to achieve a different result.

Years ago, I remember hearing a theory about how children learn about science: when children are playing, they are applying and learning scientific concepts such as cause and effect, change and variables by testing them in their games. If they have been able to do this freely as a young child, then later if they go on to study science, they will find it easy to lay the theories over the top of the hands-on learning they have already absorbed.

A child is constantly questioning and trialling, experimenting and adjusting. From repeatedly throwing food off a highchair to more serious risk-taking endeavours, a child left to explore is possibly the perfect science student. If allowed to experiment freely, a child's learning may be internalised and possibly unseen by you unless they are excited to share it with you – and then, hopefully, it is accepted, not tested.

A huge percentage of a child's play involves mucking around and learning about concepts that are science-related. Einstein understood the value of play when he said, 'Play is the highest form of research.' I would venture to say that the children I raised (the two boys in particular) were 'learning science' through practical, experimental play up to 80% of the time. Here is an example of a game of pure physics which they invented and played regularly.

DOWN THE WIRE
The boys loved this game called 'down the wire'. They tied a fishing line to a curtain rail and let the line out, pulled it tight down over two rooms, down some stairs into another room and fastened it. They had about ten metres of line starting at 2 metres high and running down at about a 45-degree angle. Onto this they would attach carabiner clips, or sometimes a paper clip or some other object of their invention. Then they would send things, usually teddies, 'down the line.' This was a fun enough game in itself; I enjoyed it too. They would then naturally want to challenge and extend themselves. It was pure physics as they discussed and trialled various weights. They would time different objects travelling from end to end, attach all sorts of things,

> including a little bag they could add items to. They even set up a second wire so they could race each other. Their conversations were all about velocity and weight and the variables that affected them: 'It might go faster if we . . . ', 'Oh that really slowed it down.' They were testing out the movement of matter through space and time which, even I know, is the definition of physics.

Other fields of science are never far away in a child's play – matter changing form when cooking, playing with fire, ice as cubes or made in much larger containers that have objects embedded in the ice. One summer Charlie and his best friend spent most of our river swimming time crushing rocks to make powders, then lugging rocks home to reduce into variously classified dust. Geologically speaking, what was the point of this? I can only guess, but their commitment to the game told me it had to be valuable, whether it was scientific, social or otherwise.

Buying some basic electronic equipment is highly recommended – wires, bulbs and switches. These items have been invaluable and were well used in our family. Children much prefer the creative potential of open-ended 'toys'. Buying an expensive electronics kit that has everything set out to be assembled to a written plan may be one option but leaving them to create something from their imagination is learning on a whole other level. For us this came in the form of years of door alarms, booby traps and various spy-related gadgets that involved lots of taping to doors and walls.

The natural world is a university in itself. No prior

knowledge or formal structure is needed to start understanding natural cycles and laws that form the basis of biology. By spending time in nature it becomes effortless to engage your skills of observation, touch, listening and tasting – which are the foundation of scientific understanding. Stargazing, especially with someone who can point out constellations and planets or explain the way the night sky changes, is priceless. We grew food from seeds, observed the moon and tides, the seasons and the weather. There are always things to look at, discover, ask about and learn from when you are outdoors in the natural world. Collecting shells, stones, leaves and fossils were all part of our lives and a reminder that living in Aotearoa New Zealand is a huge privilege.

The foundations of chemistry are surely found in the making of potions. Messy play of any description is popular with children of all ages while being calming for those with sensory issues. Paints that are mixed up instead of painted with, playdough thinned out or with various extra ingredients added becomes a gloopy mixture creating a fun way for children to experiment with texture. For the adult, this type of play is great practice to let go of your tidy gene and your expectation of how something should be played with.

If you keep providing resources, the magic will occur even in the most everyday situations. Having a bath can become a science laboratory where colours are provided (in the form of food colouring) to mix together, objects that float and sink are available, and containers for transferring water are supplied. Play that is science based will become more complex as children grow, yet without the enjoyment diminishing. Harry Potter was an inspiration for so much of our children's play, so making potions was a regular go-to activity for them.

> **POTIONS**
> Hannah had a large box full of containers of all sorts of liquids, dried plants and chopped, grated and melted substances – you name it, it was in there. Containers of all descriptions were labelled with Harry Potter ingredient names, so potions could be made according to the books. This was heaps of fun (for them) and heaps of disgusting, stinky cleaning up of often years old potions in jars (for me). Although it was pure fun for them, it was also a rich learning environment, scientifically speaking, in terms of mixing, separating, fermenting, changing, exploding, smelling and occasionally tasting.

Be assured that science is everywhere. To aid your children in having a solid grounding in the sciences, consider leaving the written, the formal and the theoretical until later on, at least the teen years, or when they indicate they are ready. Meanwhile, let them play unhindered. They will be laying the scientific base for future study without even realising it.

Chapter 9

LEARNING IS EVERYWHERE AND IN EVERYTHING

Learning is not just about reading, writing, maths and science. Children learn in all aspects of life, every day and in every way. If you wanted to analyse the learning that occurs, you could categorise their learning according to 'subject' areas. The impetus to do this may be driven by a fear that your children are not being adequately educated, but hopefully that fear will disappear as you trust natural learning more and can accept that your children are doing what they need to in any given area of learning.

A VARIETY OF SUBJECTS

The range of different topics and the ways they integrate into the lives of children are as numerous and varied as our personalities. How your children encounter music and art, history and geography in your family will depend on the experiences they have. Your attitudes to health and to physical activity will dictate their early learning. I see the role of a parent as someone who offers their children the world, laid out like a buffet. How will a person know they want to play a brass instrument if they have never seen or heard one? How does a child long to be a dancer if they never know it is a viable career option? Have they ever had a chance to paddle a canoe or roller skate? You may talk about what working in a bank entails, or what training to be a dentist or midwife involves. Perhaps your child is interested in a visiting plumber or builder, or you might discuss how local politics work during elections. There is no restriction on the number of topics you might cover, no schedule for learning about them, and no limit to your child's learning. Traditional subject areas can become blurred and melded into other subjects.

I never grouped or named topics in a way that related to the school curriculum. I simply enjoyed introducing and explaining new ideas or experiences as they arose, prompted by visitors, books and current events. Showing my children the world through experiences of live theatre and music, art, books, films and travel, was fun, to say the least. I experienced and learned alongside the kids as we explored the natural world as well as the world created by humans and the systems that govern both. It meant surrounding the children with interesting and inspiring people. I showed them as much as possible of what there was to see and do in life, then if interested, they could ask for more information or some personal experience.

TITANIC

This is a great example of how one family may be engaged in the same topic with each bringing their own perspective to it, creating a rich, multi-disciplinary learning adventure. When Hannah was six and Ollie was four years old they became hooked on the story of the Titanic. The local library had six books about this topic, which we read on repeat for four months. The children watched the film once, engrossed in the characters of Jack and Rose. We then all had to listen to 'that' song, also for four months. Hannah and Ollie often played Jack and Rose, as we each did, balancing on a pretend bow. Charlie, who was just a year old at the time, went along with whatever role was offered.

Ollie was captivated by what caused the Titanic to sink and how it split when it went down. He carried around a wooden model of the ship he had made at Playcentre which could separate in two so he could demonstrate how the ship looked when it sank. He would show strangers in the supermarket how to do this.

Hannah was interested in the people aboard. She started each day as a new character and dressed up as they would have – 'Today I am a nanny of a first-class family,' or 'I am a young girl from London who is in second class.' She wanted to know about the rules surrounding the classes and who could move between the decks. As a teacher I could have dissected and recorded the cross-curriculum learning that went on because there was plenty of it. However, I knew this analysis was unnecessary.

MONEY

Money and how it moves around in our lives provides rich learning opportunities for us all and ones that are relevant to the real world your children are living in. There are the practicalities to learn around how we relate to earning, spending, gifting and saving money. Talking about finances can also provide a deeper glimpse into ourselves and bring about occasions to discuss your own values and those of our society. The topic of money is a perfect launching pad to consider concepts of consumerism, poverty, inequality, excessive wealth and equity.

FULL MOON POCKET MONEY

It was important to me that my children had the experience of having money to use in whatever way they chose. How else would they learn about money? Our system was that they received the equivalent of their age in pocket money every full moon. It meant they could rely on the money, anticipate it, and plan for it. Working out how much pocket money you receive in a year was a good motivation to learn basic maths skills too. I had looked at systems where children were expected or encouraged to divide their money into three categories – save, spend and gift to others. I met resistance with this from myself and the kids and, as with many structured arrangements, did not pursue it. That approach seemed controlling and blocked them from feeling empowered and learning the true lessons there are to learn around money that I know I have experienced.

Your values around money will be internalised by your children, whatever they see them to be. Saying 'yes' to children does not mean that you have to buy them everything they ask for. They may be empowered to earn the money themselves or look for alternatives to what it is they desire. Valuing experiences over 'stuff' may be appreciated, as may second-hand toys and clothes, reusing and repurposing objects, and sharing or swapping toys or games with other families. Each of these ways of approaching what money can buy contains life-long lessons and helps children to understand what having, or not having, money feels like.

I have never paid the children to do jobs around the house. I gave them money so they could learn about it. Helping with jobs around the house was an expected part of our family culture. There was an assumption, based on my own experience, that by the age of 14 they would be earning their own money in some way. I certainly encouraged and supported the kids to work as they got older and, as predicted, they were all earning in some capacity by 14. My own value of earning and saving money was apparent in my children. The financial independence gained so young is empowering, especially when the money is earned yourself.

SPENDERS OR SAVERS

All three children were savers and spent their money wisely.

Hannah spent her money on books and second-hand clothes. Ollie spent his on survival, outdoor and camping gear, knives, and for a while, food to store as part of his disaster preparedness. Charlie

> used to busk on his banjo-ukulele when he was eight and nine years old, he would walk into the toy shop and empty a pile of coins onto the counter as a down payment on an expensive Lego set. He earned and spent hundreds of dollars this way and even now he owns a large amount of Lego. I would still hand over his nine dollars each month, but it felt like a drop in the ocean compared to what he was earning himself. It was no surprise that by the age of 14 he had developed his own business and by the age of 16 was working full time for himself, paying tax and renting office space.

I enjoy transparency around money and was always open about what we earned and what we spent if asked by the children. We had long discussions about how a mortgage works, what insurance does and other expenses we had. If there was a special occasion, for example a dinner they wanted to cook or tramping food to buy for a trip, there was much enjoyment and learning to be had by giving them cash and letting them wander around the supermarket to shop to a budget.

Money provides a wonderful real-life platform for learning across many conventional curriculum areas and gives you the chance to discuss bigger ideas, while learning about individual personalities, feelings and reactions around money.

FOOD

Food and the processes around eating provide a diverse range of hands-on learning experiences: from budgeting and shopping, growing, storing and preserving food, to planning, preparing, cooking, serving and eating together. Food and its preparation can be a simple yet powerful way to inspire young learners, giving them real life skills while practising maths, science, health and gardening. Apart from the practical skills children learn around food, having more time to be mindful about growing, preparing and eating it can also bring rich opportunities for you all as a family.

Relaxing meals and relaxed attitudes towards food can help children learn about the pleasures of eating, different tastes and personal preferences. Like all aspects of life as natural learners, the kids can be involved as much as they want and learning will happen, whether you intend it to or not, whatever they are doing.

Food is a big focus for many of us, especially when you have a family to care for. It can also offer plenty of scope for stress – with kids around the house all day, the mess created can easily get out of control. I find cooking relaxing and creative. A big bonus for me being at home with the kids was that I got to spend time producing good meals and we could all eat well. Whether it was me cooking and preparing food, or a child getting creative, having the time to put into preparing a meal was a hugely positive outcome of being based at home. The fact that we had no early mornings meant we could have long family dinners with no urgent rush to get to bed. The building of a simple, stress-free ritual, like a family dinner can have a big impact on your overall wellbeing and connection as a family.

I am an advocate of letting children serve themselves, as the most empowering way to learn about portion control. Recognising when they are full or have had enough is also an important skill. Alleviating any stress around food by offering a variety that they could serve themselves was an important part of natural learning for us. Learn to trust that a child will eat what they need when they are offered plenty of healthy food. If they are not pressured to eat food they don't want, this may help prevent eating disorders developing later in life.

People have different rhythms and eating speeds, so taking the time to accommodate these different paces is a supportive way to show respect to your child. If one of my children wasn't hungry, I would ask them to dish some dinner up to eat later and sit and chat with us while we ate. Taste buds change as we grow too, so not having a fixed narrative around a child's eating habits will help them be open to trying new things as their tastes change. Statements like 'Charlie hates mushrooms' or 'Hannah only eats a meal with cheese on' can easily get embedded and become a self-fulfilling prophecy for them. I found that around puberty the kids often returned from friends' homes announcing they now liked a certain food they had always disliked.

INCORPORATING FOOD INTO PLAY

Feeding other people is an act of love for me, so I often made the kids delicious, healthy food that was then delivered to where they were playing so the game did not have to be interrupted. They always appreciated this gesture, seeing it for the gift it was. Food was often incorporated into the game itself; for many years while setting up and running an 'army base', Ollie assigned me to oversee the mess tent. In an often-repeated game where the kids dressed up and were 'escaping over the mountains to Switzerland' (definite Sound of Music influence), I was the kind old lady in a cottage who gave them a basket of food. I always delighted in seeing them dressed up in 'olden day' clothes earnestly picnicking in the park next door. Their cooking enterprises over the years have seen us enjoying multi-course meals, colour-themed meals, dress-up Harry Potter-themed meals and rainbow-coloured meals. They have enjoyed preparing food to cook on an outdoor fire and planning, sorting and packing their meals for tramping trips.

Friends who are natural learners with four children have a radical and freeing system for preparing and cooking food in their home. Each person cooks what they want, when they want it. There are times when food is shared by prior agreement, but the majority of the time each person sticks to their own rhythm. The parents assure me that this system costs no more than having one person managing the kitchen. It works well in their family as the kids all enjoy cooking, the youngest has been cooking since he was two years old. It started when one morning he went out to get an egg from their chickens, came back inside and cooked it all by himself before anyone else was up. Although the kitchen is often in a state of chaos, there is less stress and a huge amount of agency, empowerment and creativity that is nurtured by the parents.

THOUGHTS ABOUT THINKING

Thinking time is a subject that is finally getting some recognition, schools are even introducing mindfulness to students. We certainly need quiet, reflective time today, with such busy lives and with so much attention demanded from online activities.

During my teacher training we were told when asking a question to the whole class to wait and not to pick the first student to put their hand up. This meant waiting for those students who needed longer to think about the question. On average I would have given them 5-10 seconds extra time, which in a busy classroom of 30 students is fairly normal. Then I learned about what thinking time was from Hannah when she was only three years old.

> ### HANNAH'S THINKING TIME
> Hannah actively claimed time to do what she called her 'thinkings' all through her childhood. Even as an adult now and an introvert she craves time alone to recharge. Her 'thinkings' were a hugely fertile ground for her imagination and when I occasionally asked what she was thinking about, I was always floored by what she told me. This also reminded me that learning is a personal and often an extremely private thing. It is no business of mine what another person needs to learn. How can I dictate what they need, where they are up to or what their curriculum should be? She continued her 'thinkings' for hours a day, often well into the night, out on the swing or the trampoline, well after we had all gone to bed.
>
> When Charlie was young, he would have a session after breakfast each day where he would lie on the sofa 'doing nothing'. Eventually I asked him what was going on and when he told me I was

truly humbled by hearing the contents of that one morning's musings. I vowed never again to doubt the power of thinking time, the capacity of a child to process all manner of things, and to invent a world of which we have no knowledge.

My advice is to let your kids be. To develop thinking skills children need time, space and quiet, and plenty of it – no screens, no parents or siblings talking to them, no time restrictions and no annoying questions about what they are doing.

BEST POSSIBLE OUTCOMES

Starting from birth, we can provide a good start for our children, with strong family relationships and an empowering, relaxing model of education conducted in a safe place, building a solid foundation that sets them up for life. 'Mindfulness' has become a catch phrase and is being used more frequently as people realise the cause of their stress and the dangers of staying too long in a 'fight or flight' mode. Adults everywhere are trying to reconnect and change old patterns of stress-inducing behaviours.

The numbers of young people with depression and anxiety are soaring around the world, and with good reason. There is plenty for us to be stressed about today – climate change, degradation of the planet, pollution, over-consumption, poverty, inequality, pandemics and wars, not to mention the usual concerns of a teenager, now amplified by social media. Children are busier than ever, with huge expectations placed on them and yet no guarantee of a secure future. We have a worldwide epidemic of mental health issues and will continue to do so unless there are some dramatic changes. If ever there was a time for a new paradigm, this is it.

Raising happy, self-reliant children is practical, time-saving and beneficial to the family and the wider community. It also develops young people who are able to lead, think creatively, work with others and tackle some of the big issues facing us all. The way we raise our children is fundamental to creating change in the world, and it is a vitally important job. Raising free thinking, natural learners could be the most impactful form of activism you could ever engage in.

What we have been doing as a human race is not working. Our human designed systems are broken and need fixing. We need to stop perpetuating the status quo and pursuing a path of disconnectedness, institutionalisation, consumerism and individualism. If we practise natural learning and raise our children to feel empowered, we may all benefit on many levels.

As natural learners practising attachment parenting, respectful communication and child centred, co-created lives, I see us at the top of the cliff shining a light to a different path. To head off some of the crises facing us we need to raise people who can be open and vulnerable, strong and resilient, heart-centred and kind. The world needs those who can think critically and are creative, brave risk-takers. We need thinkers and we need scientists as much as we need artists and change-makers. But first, we need parents to view parenting as the crucial, world-changing job that it is. In a world swirling with influences, there are no guarantees, but natural learning and respectful parenting may lead to any of the following, highly desirable qualities and outcomes:

POTENTIAL NATURAL LEARNING OUTCOMES

Self-confidence
Integrity
Perseverance
Self-awareness
Creativity
Risk-taking
Empathy
Original thinking
Cooperation

Clear communication
Self-motivation
Contentment
Heart centred living
Acceptance
Discipline

The flow-on effects of low stress, emotional security, good nutrition and plenty of sleep are far reaching and can be reason enough to slow down and free up a childhood. The long-term health benefits that follow mean that our young people will be in a better position as adults to step up as positively contributing members of society.

Chapter 10

MEASURING PROGRESS

In a school setting, measuring progress is part of a cycle where children are tested, taught specific content, then tested again to see if they have learned or retained the lesson. Even with peer or self-assessment there is an assumption that testing is a necessary part of the 'learning cycle.' However, natural learners need no formal assessment or testing to determine their prowess as learners or their progress in any given area.

If you follow the path of natural learning, external assessment becomes obsolete and superfluous. This is partly because you have fewer children than in a classroom and your own offspring are well known to you, especially if you are with them full time. You can often observe any learning that is taking place, just as you have been doing since they were born and first learned to grasp your finger.

For the most part, however, testing a child to see what they have learned is not needed. The evaluation process becomes a natural built-in response as humans grow and develop, so your child will be self-monitoring their progress instinctively. As a young toddler your child didn't stop once they had mastered crawling or standing. They continuously assessed their progress, realised there was more to learn and moved onto the next stages of walking, climbing and running, instinctively challenging themselves as they developed.

If a child is allowed to follow their own interests and rhythms, and if their inquiring nature is met with support and love, they will extend themselves naturally. When a child is exposed to the world around them and experiences a variety of people and places, engaging their senses, their intellect or their body, they process each situation and decide for themselves what they do next. Their response may be anything from 'This is strange/scary/boring/I am not interested in this' to 'Wow, I love the look of that and want to try it' – and everything in between.

Personal learning styles will also become apparent to you as a parent. You will observe whether your child prefers to spend time looking at others before trying something themselves or takes their time to think about a new idea or situation. Some children are visual or kinesthetic learners, some prefer auditory methods to gain new information. Once you understand this, you will realise how unfair it is to have a universal way of educating children and any 'one size fits all' testing. As the popular saying, often accredited to Einstein, goes: 'Everybody is a genius. But if you judge a fish by its ability to climb a tree, it will spend its whole life thinking it is stupid.'

When learning naturally, a person's achievement comes through self-motivation and does not need to be tested, shared or compared with anyone else. When you know yourself well and can take your own time to do what you want, being tested on someone else's schedule seems a strange idea. A child will ask if they do not know something. They naturally want to learn what is next. They are born to learn – at their own pace. They do not need to be tested to see if they have retained any knowledge. If it is knowledge or a skill that is of interest to them or used regularly, then, just like an adult, there is a good chance it will be retained. If, like square root, it is something that you hardly ever use (in my case) then why would you need to retain that knowledge?

Our personal knowledge changes as we grow, depending on how often we use it. I certainly do not remember all the things I crammed for my exams at university. If I wanted to remind myself of something I studied years ago, I would use the skills I have to look it up – read a book or Google it. I am grateful to have the skills to do this. Skills are what a person learns when they repeatedly practise something – walking, playing an instrument or a sport, cooking or driving. For a child these are the skills they develop through playing and repeating as much as they need.

SCHEMA

Throughout their life a child will develop and work on schemas. These are repeated patterns around a theme. A child will set them up for themselves so they can explore that pattern in different ways. You can usually see what they are practising and you will learn to recognise the schema they are in. I see schema as a child's own in-built assessment system. They keep extending themselves and practising until they understand the concept and have explored all its facets – then they move on. There are various types of schema that are recognised and used as guides to a young child's behaviour.

> **HERE ARE SOME COMMON SCHEMA:**
> - *Connecting* – Joining toys together, vehicles and trailers, using lots of sellotape or nails, or holding hands to make lines
> - *Orientation* – Turning things around, puzzles, changing perspective, being upside down
> - *Transporting* – moving things from place to place, perhaps in toy vehicles or bags
> - *Trajectory* – dropping things or throwing things, falling and jumping
> - *Positioning* – arranging things is a particular way, lining things up, ordering them
> - *Enveloping* – hiding, covering up, dressing up, putting things in bags and wrapping up gifts.
> - *Enclosing* – building walls or fences in play, marking edges and boundaries
> - *Rotation* – making circles by using their bodies to spin around, circling their limbs, placing toys in circles, drawing circles and creating circles with toys.

This is a way that a child self-monitors and only they know when they are ready to move on. There are no timeframes attached to schema, it is an individualised and internalised system.

No parent or teacher can ever know if a child has finished all they need to know in one schema area, so trying to control a child's play interferes with their natural system of evaluation. Adults often only see the external manifestation of a child's play and of the schema they are working in. A common concern of parents is to think their child is spending too much time in one place or playing one thing. Their concern is often based on their own fears or needs and has nothing to do with what their child is learning. I have heard comments from concerned parents about their child who 'has spent eight months playing only in the sandpit and needs to get out and do something else.' But if you look more closely at what the child has been playing in the sandpit, you will see the progression and development of their play and how it has become more complex as various schemas have been worked through. The sandpit was just a fun and familiar place to practise what was needed.

PROOF OF LEARNING

I saw an advertisement for after-school tutoring recently which read: 'We know that your child is a genius, we just help them prove it.' It perfectly illustrated what we don't do as natural learners. It may be tempting to seek proof of what your child has learned, but that is your own fear speaking and expectations coming through that you need to let go of.

Parents often want to prove what their children know, especially to other people. This testing of babies and toddlers is commonplace as you want to share the miracle of their natural learning with visitors. Many of us have found ourselves asking our toddler, 'What does a dog say?

or 'Show so-and-so how you can count,' or 'What colour is that toy?' If the child knows the answer, then how silly making them tell you; if they don't know, then they may feel stupid or ashamed for not performing correctly.

The same principle applies to older children and to adults. If you treat your child as you would like to be treated, then you wouldn't continually test them. As adults, we don't challenge our friends socially to display a newly learned skill or test them on current events. Why should we expect our children to perform in that way? If a child knows something and it serves them at the time, then that's fine – they will use it for as long as they need to.

I knew many of the things I talked about with the kids as they were growing up were of transitory interest. When a child was interested in something, questions would flow, and they were totally focused and fascinated, just as I am in new situations. This did not mean that they would remember everything we spoke about. It meant that they each took from the conversation whatever was relevant to them at the time. I love how, even now, we can recall a shared experience and yet all remember it in wildly varying ways.

AT THE ART GALLERY

We went to see the Impressionists, an art exhibition from Europe. I was happy to wander around taking in the art. Hannah wandered and chatted with my mum, Charlie was five years old, so I showed him various parts of paintings I thought he would relate to. It was an inspiring collection of famous paintings. When we had finished and exited the exhibition, I

> noticed that Ollie's eyes were shining, and he could barely control his eight-year-old excitement. He then shared with us his experience – the exact number of security cameras, the positioning and movements of the security guards, the exits, the alarms. He was ignited with the buzz of figuring out how someone might steal one of those priceless paintings and how well they were protected. He talked at great length about what he had seen and how he had worked out various scenarios. The art? I don't think he even looked at a painting. This was a defining moment and a great lesson for me to have no expectations about what another person learns and takes away from an experience.

Children show us constantly how they retain what is relevant to them on their journeys. Hannah knew the seven Harry Potter books verbatim and would call out a missed adjective from another room when I was reading aloud to the boys. It is fascinating to see what they each remembered in different situations and then again over time. I could so easily have had preconceived ideas of what their takeaway 'should' have been and even tested them on it in any given situation. To them this would have seemed irrelevant and annoying, as it would have been what I thought or perceived as important, what I wanted, and had little or no relevance to them or their learning.

NO BOOK WORK

There is no requirement for natural learners to keep any sort of record of learning for your child. However, you may want to record their childhood experiences in some way, as any parent does. There are many interesting and creative systems parents have set up to have a record of what fills the years of childhood. Some people do nothing concrete or organised while others produce photo books or similar. If you like to take photos or write about what you do as a family or what individual children do for your own interest, you may be doing this anyway.

I have heard of parents who set up an email account for their child and email it each week, or month with photos and news about what they have been saying, doing and experiencing. The plan is to then give the email address and password to the child when they turn 18. Maybe you could take a photo at the same spot each year, make videos, save birthday cards and little love notes from your children – you are limited only by your imagination when deciding how, and if, to record a childhood in concrete terms.

A RECORD OF A CHILDHOOD

I have kept clearfiles for the kids, which I have enjoyed filling over the years. Each child has ended up with several bulging folders they still love to look at. I regularly took photos and would write up explanations, keep tickets or programmes and stick them all in. Each was a labour of love providing some creative expression for me and a celebration of that child, their life and discoveries. Sometimes they wrote things, but mostly they loved seeing what I put together and they were grateful for such a grand record of themselves.

While assessment and testing can greatly interfere with a person's learning journey, there are times where it occurs in our lives – for example, taking a driving test, or as a part of an extracurricular activity. Music and dancing exams, martial art gradings and sporting competitions are all commonplace. Some people shy away from these regulated activities while others swear by competition from a young age. Your own personal values and your child's interests in activities are the only guide necessary. However, it is entirely possible to raise a well-balanced and happy child without any testing or external assessment.

Chapter 11

SETTING LIMITS WITH TECHNOLOGY

Screen time is for me a parenting issue, and not one that is particular to those educating at home. But as natural learners we have more time to engage in every activity, including time online. Easy access to material online inevitably raises questions about how much to monitor and restrict, and how to implement that in a family where children are allowed to 'do what they want'.

This is a complicated and relatively new issue for parents, teachers and caregivers. Being on a computer for long periods of time is something that currently affects many young people. It can be a contentious issue, and I can only offer my observations, which will no doubt differ greatly from the values and experiences of other families. I know from conversations at natural learners camps, conferences and get-togethers that concerned parents are constantly asking 'How much screen time is OK?'

I have met children as young as eight who cannot play imaginative games, only online ones. This saddens me and sets alarm bells ringing. The effects of the huge amount of screen time that children are currently exposed to is unknown. Schools are embracing computers more and more as a regular way to work. In Aotearoa New Zealand we have a new and compulsory digital technology curriculum for children aged 7 and over. I see this as unnecessary and have concerns about children spending the bulk of their day on a device. The school work I have witnessed primary aged students doing does not need to be on a computer. There seems to be a lot of work on a computer for the sake of it, not the necessity. The effects in a class of constant screen time brings about a marked decrease in interaction with others and a reliance on the internet which I can only see as unhealthy.

Recently I was working in a school, teaching 11- and 12-year-olds, and as I am interested in technology use I asked them a lot of questions. Some young students spent every waking hour, when not at school, playing online games. I have had students tell me they 'game' until 4am on school nights, which meant they were so tired they couldn't think straight and were barely awake in class. Most classes had between two and five of these compulsive gamers who could not talk about anything else – the games were their whole lives. These kids were lacking basic social skills, such as having a conversation, interacting and asking questions. Some children told me all their schoolwork was on a device now and that their eyesight became so bad they needed glasses. Many of the young people lacked basic practical skills and had no exposure to making or creating in a hands-on way, while others said they didn't cook meals or help out at home.

Extended time on a computer raises the concern of

physical development and the issue of sitting for so long while backs, necks and legs are all growing. Are we not designed to be active for large parts of the day? The worldwide obesity epidemic is attributed to poor diet and lack of exercise, and the hours of inactivity in front of a screen are surely a contributing factor.

A huge and growing area of concern, on which I do not pretend to be an expert, is mental health. Online bullying, the influence of social media and readily available pornography are some of the highly profiled dangers for young people. Strong and enduring relationships will go a long way in helping children grow up resilient in today's world. Natural learning is the perfect opportunity to forge great relationships and have time to talk through the problems that arise from these and other complex issues.

The availability of technology feels like an unstoppable tidal wave and I feel grateful to have raised my children in a TV-free house, where we only got the internet as they became teenagers. My overriding concern is the lack of time spent playing, which I see as vital to developing young brains and bodies. Although people assure me that many online games are interactive and engage the brain in similar ways to hands-on, real life playing, I am not convinced of this. There are concerns around the content being viewed, values being absorbed, advertising and the potential for addiction. The internet is a part of everyday life for most of us and while accepting that I still would advocate for minimum screen time for children.

HOW WE DID THE INTERNET

The internet and its use among my growing children caused me stress, as it did for many of my friends and other parents worldwide. I have mixed feelings about it still and am lucky that now our children all have full lives outside of their phones. There is no doubt there was plenty of time wasted on the internet, and still is, by them all. We talk about this, but luckily they are self-aware and are happy to go away to wilderness areas without phone service and enjoy it.

I took a risk when we got the internet. At the time the kids were aged eight, 11 and 13, and although I did monitor and restrict their use until they were teenagers, I then let them regulate their own use after this. This happened with constant pressure from me to get outside and to do something else – a manifestation of my own fear of what long hours online would cause and what they were missing out on, alongside my fingers-crossed-behind-my-back approach. I did not enjoy them being on a device, and I did not enjoy having to police a rule. It felt like a minefield, yet I decided to trust them and hold onto the conviction that they would learn for themselves how to self-manage. This did indeed happen, and still does periodically as they take steps to reduce their online time and change their habits.

The consequences of the huge disconnect from the natural world are yet to be known, and it's something that keeps me awake at night. When out at the beach or a park on a sunny weekend I wonder where the young people are. If children have no connection to nature, what hope do we have for them to care enough to help protect and regenerate the damage to our planet? How many children can light a fire? How many can forage, build a shelter or grow food?

Having met many young people who cannot even tie a knot, I feel these concerns are not unfounded. This is a vast topic which will provide debate for some time yet. Surely the tide will soon turn as parents realise their kids need to be outside, taking risks and engaging with the natural world and some balance will return to those who have lost it.

OLDER CHILDREN

As children grow into young adults, increased use of the internet is almost a given. As a tool for learning, for communication or for creative expression, natural learners are often adept users of digital technology, like most young people. It would be an exception to have teenagers who do not engage in online activities, and there are many life-expanding, positive and helpful opportunities to be had for them. The internet is an incredible tool that can bring the world to a natural learner. The trick is to balance screen-based activities with real life, face-to-face experiences.

OUR POSITIVE STORIES

In amongst the mindlessness and time wasting, the kids used the internet to their advantage as teenagers: Hannah wrote fanfiction and studied for her NCEA qualifications; Ollie had a YouTube channel for his dozens of survival videos and listened to podcasts about everything from politics to chemistry; Charlie shared Lego stop motion films he created, which then morphed into his video content business.

I enjoy hearing how parents manage and balance screen use with family time, exercise and other interests. A parent can only do their best. Personally, I see an ideal childhood up to puberty, as being screen free, but achieving this is becoming increasingly difficult. What can we do except keep being the change and modeling what we want to see. We may try to hide the router periodically, have screen free days or go away into the wilderness where there is no internet. These strategies allow us all to have breaks, whatever our age. Unless you are clear that you want to go without the internet, then embarking on the full time parenting of your children can be a good time to work out a new 'normal' for time online and to prioritise what is important in your household.

Chapter 12

NAVIGATING THE TEENAGE YEARS

The teenage years are often thought of as challenging. But these years can be wonderful in many ways, too. This stage of parenting can be a magical time of empowering change for all, a time of fledgling independence not just for the young people, but for their parents too. Older children can share some of the responsibilities of running the household, allowing you to take more time out for yourself. The new influences, new friends and new questions that flow into your lives can enrich your family and offer more learning than ever in new and unimagined directions.

Yet why do teens get such bad press in our culture? It is a testing time for a young person as they face huge changes. With so much still to learn, a teenager can feel confused and vulnerable, especially as they venture away from the security of home and family more often.

When Charlie was 13 he said to me, 'Mum we are pretty much going through the same crazy, hormone fuelled-stage.' I was perimenopausal, which is also known as second puberty, and hearing this helped to equalise us and reminded me that we all have seasons in our lives to weather.

COMMUNICATION

Although it may not seem like it at times, teenagers still need you. A teenager needs to be able to communicate in their own time and in their own way, and for that to happen they need a parent present, both physically and emotionally. The need for you, or another adult they respect, is just as important now as in the toddler years. The challenge is that they need you in a different way and at different times, and as the parent you will have to be the one to recognise what this looks like. Learning to listen, if you have not already, will serve you well at this stage of the parenting journey. By listening and accepting, not judging or offering unasked for advice, you can help provide a safe place for your teenager to talk about their life.

> ### LESSONS FROM TEENAGERS
> I am blessed to have been a mum to two wonderful kids through their teenage years when I joined the family. I learned some important lessons about parenting teens during this time, while I was adding three more babies to our family. One of the biggest revelations was that teens still need their parents. I noticed that every day between getting home from school and having dinner each of them would come and find me – usually cooking and juggling babies, and tell me something, unprompted, about their

day. It may have been an angry verbal outburst, it may have been barely a few words, but they sought out that connection. I am so glad that I was able to be there for them, doing the best I could do as a relatively new mum myself.

Young people need your time and your accepting, supportive and unconditional love. This can be hard to continue in the same way as when they were younger. It is common for teens to want to break away from the family in some way, with varying degrees of desperation or urgency. This can look and sound like they hate or resent you and be upsetting after raising them lovingly for years. Your parenting can be thrown back in your face and you can feel alienated from your child for the first time since they were born. This new stranger in their place may bear no resemblance to your little toddler of a decade ago. As a parent there can be much distress and grief and a desire to hang on to your baby for as long as possible.

This is sometimes a harsh transition to adulthood, for all involved and it seems to be aggravated by too much dominance on the parent's part. Many factors can contribute to the conflicts that may arise, but controlling parenting will commonly push young people underground or away. As parents, we need to change the way we treat our young people as they grow. The way we viewed them and treated them as young children no longer serves them. They need to be given more agency and more independence. The trust we had in them as a five- or six-year-old, lighting a fire or climbing trees must be extended into more adult domains. By trusting them, you have the best chance of keeping the communication lines open, which is paramount. Parenting that is seen as controlling by a young person can push them further away and result in lies and deception. If the communication is still flowing between parent and teenager, then you have more prospect of connecting with them and getting across messages of safety and of your unconditional love and support. It may be hard to hear that your 16-year-old was drunk, but how grateful you must be to have heard it and know they are still sharing this information with you.

MAKING THE TRANSITION

With no clear delineation of where childhood ends and adulthood begins, the teenage years can be confusing. Many cultures have a traditional coming of age ceremony or rite of passage to mark this change and support a child into adulthood, but often the transition goes unmarked in our society. Instead, teenagers face a demand to perform academically, social pressure magnified by social media, and an uncertain future which can feel overwhelming, given the problems facing our planet.

Advice to parents of young children is to let your children play as much as possible, for when they reach a certain stage in their development, often around puberty, their capacity for imaginative play will slow down and cease. This can be sad for a parent and like all endings you will need time to deal with the grief that arrives. The changes in your child may be sudden or may fluctuate as they waver between childhood and the adult world. Childhood, with its rich imaginative life, is replaced by a realisation that they will step out into the world and take their place in it.

SUDDEN OUTWARD CHANGE

For Hannah, there was a definite line drawn in the sand, a single day where she considered herself to have moved on and crossed over. Over the course of a single day she emptied her bedroom out of childhood toys as she recognised the great change in herself. She put her large doll's house, full of things she considered a part of her childhood, with several boxes in the hallway, and asked me to 'please get rid of them.' This was a powerful event to witness and it was such an honour as a parent to be part of the transition.

The first part of childhood is inward looking, when a child has their imagination intact and extremely active. This is the time when they are absorbing all the information they experience in the world around them. Ideally, this is a time of having a secure life where their needs are met and they are loved and supported unconditionally. In the teen years, they begin to look outwards. They develop a curiosity about the role they will take on in life, accompanied by excitement or apprehension, eagerness or anxiety. It is a big time of change, no matter how they feel or what they choose to do. They are looking at the world differently and contemplating how they will fit into it. A teenager is deciding what resonates with them in the adult world as they start replacing their play with real life. They begin to think in practical, concrete terms about what they will do, how they will do it and what skills they want to learn or develop.

DEVELOP A RITE

Many cultures have a rite of passage for a young person to celebrate their transition into adulthood. In Aotearoa New Zealand, some thoughtful movements are emerging to create a new paradigm. Tracks (for boys) and Tides (for girls) provide an intensive rite, where in small groups, with many adult and young adult supporters a young person gets to celebrate who they are. This established programme provides a five-day experience for a young person and a parent or supportive adult. The young people move through a rite of passage developed to increase a sense of their unique self and their confidence while celebrating their new status as an adult with the accompanying rights and responsibilities.

If there is nothing official available to you and your own children, then think about developing something to celebrate and mark this time of transition. It may be a special trip with a parent, a ceremony with friends or a quiet one-on-one time to talk over what is being left behind. A significant gift to mark the transition can be a meaningful way to honour your child.

The transition to adulthood happens over many years, covering many stages of growth in a person's physical, mental and emotional development. As in every other stage in life, natural learning can help make it an innate transition in a safe, supportive environment.

REBELLION

Rebellion is a word commonly associated with teenagers. But what is rebellion, other than reaching for and testing out of the next stage? Perhaps this is how moving away and becoming more independent looks like to your teenager.

Just as for the younger child, there is a strong need for an older child to make the learning their own. The learning can, however, involve scarier things now that they are older and out of the home more. The new influences on our children can make us parents feel uncomfortable and nervous.

We know that in puberty a young person's brain is changing and developing. They have a need to push boundaries as they continue to explore. What is seen as 'rebellion' is part of growing up and finding your own path in life. A young person may eventually return to the values and lifestyle they were raised in, but via a meandering path of self-discovery. The learning of bigger life lessons needs to be made through the lens of practical experience. While well-meaning parents may try to warn their children not to make the same mistakes they themselves made, simply hearing advice is not always the way to truly learn. A wise adult knows to nod and smile accepting their child's journey of discovery and supporting them without the no desire to say 'I told you so' years later.

REBELS

A running joke for emerging teens in our house was trying to find something to rebel against. They listed things to test out my boundaries. Can I get a tattoo? Yes. Can I get piercings? Yes. Dye my hair? Yes. None of these happened. The kids were also raised as vegetarians, and it came as no surprise when Ollie wanted to start eating meat as a young teenager. I was prepared and accepted this as part of who he was. A friend of ours offered to show

> him how to kill a chicken, which he did, then he prepared and cooked it. There was no rebellion.

Rebellion will look different depending on your family culture and the values you have. Many natural learners have a relaxed and open lifestyle with their children, so rebellion may be hard to spot or even be non-existent. In many families there is no great transition, not even leaving home, just a close family that continues living together as children become adults. The amount of negotiation needed to live together like this will depend on the expectations of the parents. Respect and communication are hopefully well developed by this stage, so the young person can grow into an adult, maintaining the freedom to be their own unique person.

HOW NATURAL LEARNING MAY HELP

The teenage years are an exciting stage of life and can completely change your family on many levels. Many new dynamics emerge, brought about by surging hormones and much personal growth. It can be a stressful time for a young person, with confusion and self-doubt reigning. Living the life of natural learning may help them get through this period with relative ease.

Firstly, there are the quality relationships that being home-based throughout your offspring's childhood has hopefully given you both. The years together with hours of quality, easy, low-stress time will have aided the deep bond which will now truly serve you as a parent. By now you will probably have established communication channels and shared responsibilities within the family. You need to trust that on some level your child knows how much you love them and have supported them through their childhood, even if they don't always show it.

Secondly, being a teenager who can choose to remain home-based as much as they want to also seems safe, emotionally, physically and mentally. They have the freedom to explore or to stay at home as and when they need to. A young natural learner is not going to be so easily pushed into uncomfortable situations. They are less likely than their school-going friends to succumb to exam pressure or peer pressure or to fulfil other social expectations until they are ready, if at all. It can be an awkward time and what is required of you as a parent is your continuing sensitivity, compassion, care and love towards them as they find their way.

> **BEING 14**
> I remember a friend telling me she was at a party and when dinner was served a woman disappeared outside with a plate of food, then returned and filled a plate for herself and ate it. Later she took a plate of dessert outside and returned with an empty dinner plate. When someone eventually asked what she was doing, she replied, 'Oh, my 14-year-old is in the car.' Those who had teenagers just nodded and smiled.

It is impossible to generalise about how the teenage years will be, with different developmental ages and stages, varying family situations and personalities all playing a part. A person's early childhood experiences and their relationship with their parents will shape and influence a young person, too. However, making the transition through the teenage years can be just as wonderful as the toddler years. My image of parenting teens is of a stretchy umbilical cord, letting them control how far they go and when they need to bounce back, with reminders that your love is unconditional and you are on their side, no matter what. I still advocate saying 'yes' to teens, just as when they were younger. I believe a young person needs to feel empowered to know they can do something, if they want.

You may also consider having an emergency word, like a code word between you and your young teen. This can be used by them to signal if they are uncomfortable in a situation and need your help to exit safely and without losing face. Perhaps you go to collect your teen from a friend's home and their friend wants your child to stay for a sleepover. Your teen really wants to be at home with you, but feels uncomfortable telling their friend this. So they can use an agreed signal or word to let you know their wishes and you can step in. As a young teenager, especially making new friends out of your social circles and having new experiences, knowing there is an 'out' can be as comforting for them as it is for you.

> **IT'S TOUGH BEING AN ADOLESCENT**
> Hannah, who had a dream life, found being 13 and 14 difficult. How was this remotely possible, when she'd had free reign to design her own life and do what she wanted all day? She stopped coming out with us anywhere and even spent a year not eating meals with us. She was in her room and in her own world. She was never pressured to do anything she didn't want to. This was her way of coping with

> the massive changes in herself, processing how she felt and how she viewed life. Hannah shared how hard it was coping with the changes that puberty brought about as she matured and settled into her young adult self and I am glad she was supported safely at home during this time. Since emerging from her little bubble, she has been fully engaged with life and all it has to offer. Maybe those two quiet years were what she needed to transition through to adulthood? When just 14 years old she spontaneously ended up spending a year living in Switzerland, going to school (and being educated in German), and travelling in Europe. Upon her return she was full of confidence and life direction.

Natural learning and the years you have spent together as a family can act as a buffer or a kind of insurance for you all as your children grow into adulthood. Natural learning provides no guarantees for a smooth passage into adulthood, as each person makes their own way in life, but wherever your teen's path takes them, hopefully they will feel supported by the trust and solid foundations established when they were young.

LETTING GO

It may seem impossible that your young child will ever grow up and want to leave you. Remember when your eight-year-old told you they want to live with you forever? Sadly, moving out and moving on is the natural way of things, although it can take several years of coming and going before you feel as though they have left. Transitioning to a life free of day-to-day parenting responsibilities is another huge topic in itself – terrifying and sad yet empowering at the same time.

The teenage years can be a time of such wonder – to see your baby stepping out and beginning to build their adult life, you can be bursting with pride one minute then sobbing with grief the next. For a parent, this is the time to make sure that you have things in place for yourself, while still being available for your young adults. If you have given your all to your children as they have grown, it can be hard to imagine them leaving the life you have built together. It can be near to impossible to start to think what you will do without them and the meaning they have brought to your life for so long.

Hopefully as a parent you can grow as your children do, creating a child-free life, which can soften the transition for you all. It is a time to begin weaving your own interests into your busy family life and creating space for yourself outside the lives of the children, so you are not left with an empty feeling when they finally leave the nest. Dovetailing hobbies, friends and other pursuits into your life with teenagers is a sensible way forward.

FROM LITTLE STEPS TO THE EXTREME

I prepared for the time my children would head off into the world by having a personal narrative where for years I would say to myself, 'One day they will go to McDonalds.' I never took them to places like that, but knew it was part of their journey to go off and explore all the world had on offer, including fast food joints. This phrase was a euphemism for the many new things they would try and do as they matured. Repeating the phrase to myself while they were still at home was a way of consciously reminding myself of the changes ahead and helped me make the adjustment once they left home. Still, having an empty nest is an enormous change of lifestyle with lots of emotional ups and downs. To mark my own transition to having an empty nest, I sold my house, quit my job and took off to walk the length of Aotearoa New Zealand on Te Araroa, the long pathway. An extreme, yet perfectly fitting celebration for me.

Our teenagers are simply young people learning about the world on a continuum from when they were born. You may feel at times that life is all on their terms, and sometimes that is just how it has to be. The hard times are hopefully matched by the good as you learn to parent differently while continuing to love them unconditionally. Maybe the frustrations you feel towards them over their selfishness is a natural mechanism to help you feel happier about them leaving home. Whatever your experience with your teenage child, remember it will pass. As your relationship with your child changes into that of two adults, it can become one that is fulfilling and loving.

Chapter 13

GAINING FORMAL QUALIFICATIONS

If a child has never been to school, many pathways are open to them if they wish to pursue a more formal education at some stage. A key belief as a natural learner, one you learn reasonably early on, is that we are all lifelong learners. This is especially true today, when people have several different careers, training is available online from anywhere with an internet connection, and jobs are changing constantly.

In the past, if a person had not learned everything by the age of 18 or 20, the view was that opportunities were closed to them. Nothing is further from the truth in my view. I always encourage young people to have some time off, go travelling, try new things, explore who they are and what they want to do next. Deciding to take up a path of formal tertiary study at any age is a commitment that is best supported by a strong desire to do so.

When you are ready to study or learn a new skill and are excited about the prospect, then it is possible to pursue this path at any stage in life. Readiness and excitement are the best prerequisites for learning. If I woke up tomorrow with a burning passion to become an astro-physicist, I would return to study and do it through sheer determination and hard work, because I am intrinsically motivated to do so.

The same goes for our children and our teenagers. Let them be – let them do what they need to, when they need to. They have all their lives to study, to learn in a formal setting and to try new things. They can go to school, to university or study online at any time they want and at any age. As they mature and are exposed to outside influences, passions and personalities, a young person may discover a whole new part of themselves and head off on an unpredictable journey of discovery.

I have met many parents of young children who are on the natural learning journey and are already worrying about how their six- or seven-year-old will get into university. This seems to be a huge area of concern for some people. They are confused and unsure about how their children will be able to operate as adults. How will they ever be prepared to study or get qualified? The question reveals an underlying fear about how their children will get on in the world as natural learners.

PRACTICAL WAYS FOR NATURAL LEARNERS TO ENTER TERTIARY STUDY
(Aotearoa New Zealand specific)
- Go to school at 15 or 16 to get the necessary NCEA qualifications.
- Enrol in Te Kura from the age of 16 to 19 – it is free for young people to study online

> with Te Kura (Te Aho o Te Kura Pounamu), traditionally known as the Correspondence School.
> - Take a bridging course offered by universities for students without high school qualifications.
> - A discretionary university entrance is available, often used by homeschooled students. A registered teacher needs to sign off a piece of written work by the student, confirming they are working at the required level to enter university.
> - Study at an institute that does not require any entry qualifications to demonstrate the ability to work at that level, then use that qualification to progress to university level study, for example a UCOL or similar.

This is my view of the public education system in a nutshell – that a group of people in authority have decided on a small body of knowledge that is required by all young people. This body of knowledge is then taught, the student is tested, and if they succeed, they are defined as 'educated' in the school system. The public education system is just one way, and by no means the only way, to acquire an education. Natural learners have a huge range of ideas, skills and paths they follow. I can only relate those I have been a part of.

In my experience of natural learning, young people around the age of 15 to 17 want to make sure that they know what their school-going peers know. They want to fit in and follow a well-trodden path. They want to ensure they can conform and can go to university via the regular route, not 'some hippy way' (direct quote from my children). What follows here are my natural learners' teenage education stories.

HANNAH'S STORY

At 16 years of age Hannah enrolled in Te Kura (the Correspondence School), a huge, well-resourced online school in Aotearoa New Zealand for remote learning. She took control of her learning, told them exactly what she wanted to achieve and sped through the absolute minimum requirements to get into university. She found out that what I had been telling her for years ('it's not rocket science') was true. She found the content of the courses easy and she completed it quickly. She wanted nothing unusual, just easy entrance into tertiary study. Hannah gained level three in History, Classics, German and English. She worked at a bookshop while she did this and then headed off travelling at 18 for two years before returning to university.

OLLIE'S STORY

Ollie was at a loose end socially when he was around 15 years of age. He was involved in Scouts, Cadets and Taekwondo, and excelled in each, going as far as he could. It concerned me that his social needs were not being met, so one day after attending a concert at our local high school (we were hosting several exchange students during this time) I had a brainwave and rushed home to tell Ollie – he should go to school, and I was sure he would love it. I just knew he was ready. He agreed and went to school for two years. For an extrovert like him, the social side was the main benefit. He had a blast. He seemed to get to know everyone within weeks and they all loved him. In his second and last year, Ollie was made Deputy Head Boy. As part of his responsibilities, he was involved with the international students. That year he had three trips to Asia with the school, making more and more friends and connections wherever he went. I hardly saw him study during those two years and to this day I don't know what he achieved academically. He said he didn't quite pass everything but did not seem too worried about it. Just as when he was a Lego-playing eight-year-old, his education was his own business. At the age of 20 and after spending time travelling, Ollie went to university to study towards a nursing degree and began training as a medic for the part-time army reserves.

CHARLIE'S STORY

Although all three of my homeschooled children had been interested in filmmaking at various times and to various extents, when Charlie hit puberty he transitioned from Lego playing and started to make stop-motion films. Since then, he has grown a video/filmmaking business that he works full time in. He is self-motivated, self-taught and self-directed. He re-invests money earned into photography equipment. He is a competent networker and appears to know a huge range of people in the business, nationwide. He makes films for local businesses, politicians, a national magazine and local projects of various descriptions. His work sees him live-streaming funerals and taking wedding videos. He has even won an award for a documentary. He seeks mentors in our community, helps support other young filmmakers, and has a pool of friends to help when needed. When developing his own 'passion project' he writes, produces, directs, films and edits the whole thing. The morphing from childhood to this confident young man, heading off to meetings and sending out invoices, has been an absolute privilege to observe and be a part of.

Interestingly, before the children became teenagers, I wrote this in my journal: 'The perfect natural learning model I can imagine is where a childhood passion develops naturally in the teen years. What may have been a game for a six- or eight-year-old becomes a full-time hobby or even a business for a 14- or 16-year-old.' Charlie's story would be the ultimate happy ending for a natural learner in many people's minds. It is an excellent way for others to see how 'successful' natural learning can be. Although I only want my children to be happy and kind in their lives, Charlie's story in particular illustrates the potential of young people who are encouraged to forge their own path.

Chapter 14

FEELING THE JOY

Choosing to have children and then embracing natural learning offers ample opportunity for joy. Children are naturally joyful and remind us of the fun to be had every day. They pull you back to the present and keep you grounded in times of stress. Children are experts at seeing and feeling delight. They call for your attention, insisting that you are fully present and bear witness to their excitement. You see and hear it in their spontaneous laughter, their smiles, their concentration and their exclamations: 'Look at this shell, Mum!', 'Come and look at what I made', 'Watch me do this!'

Being a natural learner is an attitude. If you can apply this frame of mind to raising your kids, in whatever way you are able, the wonder and joy will enrich all your lives. To sit amongst your children while they climb on you, run around, perform to you, talk to you or hug you is surely a feeling of ultimate joy. To see the wonderful, the hilarious and the miraculous in the ordinary, as they do, through their eyes is a gift in itself. Being blessed with children feels like a privilege. By creating time to truly enjoy them as they grow is the ultimate tribute to them, and to yourselves as parents.

Growing children remind us how fleeting and transitory life is. Precious moments must be seized, not relegated to the 'one day' list. There is no 'one day', there is only now, for by tomorrow your child will have grown and changed yet again. The special time that natural learning opens up in your lives allows you to honour the sacredness of childhood. This may be in simplest of ways – lying and reading together for hours on end, cooking together or wandering around the neighbourhood chatting.

SHARING YOUR BLISS

When you spend so much time together, you will get to share in their exuberance and with any luck will feel plenty of your own. We can all choose to spend some time engaged in things that bring a smile to our faces. We can choose to react with joy and to see the fun in everyday moments. We can appreciate our child's enthusiasm and share it with them simply by stopping and being present in that moment.

Natural learning provided me with the time to slow down and appreciate what I had around me. I became adept at practising gratitude and at seeing the beauty in the smallest of things. By being able to live my best life and feel fulfilled, I could share my favourite things with the kids. The joy then flowed both ways. Just as I shared in their joy when they were happy doing what they wanted, they would share in my happiness when we were adventuring or doing something that really topped me up.

> **SHARING ADVENTURES**
>
> Combining two of my favourite things – my children and adventuring – meant I was living my bliss every time we went anywhere. Mostly this was when we went camping or tramping or did road trips to stay with family. Yet a local walk where we would light a spontaneous fire or build a hut was just as much fun. Attending music festivals where I was relaxed and happy meant I was present with the kids, while filling up my own cup. This was a win-win for me as a parent.
>
> Our first shared overseas experience was attending an unschooling conference in Australia. We had to borrow money to fund this, long since paid back, but we still recall the many special moments of this trip, appreciating the fun and magic of being in the company of so many like-minded folk. The shared challenges became humorous after a while or evolved into epic tales to be told later, time and again.
>
> Heading off overseas for nearly five months with three kids aged nine, 12 and 14, one small backpack each and a banjolele was a dream realised for me. This trip created a bounty of shared memories that strengthened our relationships. We spent a month backpacking around Turkey, and visited friends in Switzerland, where Hannah ended up spontaneously staying for a year and going to school. We camped and stayed with family in the UK. Couch surfing in each country provided a unique way to meet local

people. We had several Harry Potter-influenced experiences in the UK, being huge fans of the novels. We returned via a week in Paris, and the boys and I had a week in Bali before coming home. Travel offers huge learning opportunities and benefits: seeing how different people live, eating different food, seeing grand and historic sights, and listening to and speaking in different languages. Our highlights were the people we met and spent time with, which reinforced my belief that as humans we have more in common than differences, and that there are kind and good people everywhere.

Travelling together with different-aged kids meant each of us brought a different perspective to the experience. The stories of that trip are woven into our lives together. I was still a full-time parent and a 'meeter of needs' while we were travelling, and I ensured that each child got to do what they wanted as much as possible. My happiness at travelling spilled over to the children and how they perceived what was happening. Doing what I enjoyed, adventuring, created a win-win situation. My cup was constantly being filled up, and as a result I was a better parent – which meant the kids were happy and the cycle was self-sustaining.

While this trip was fun in innumerable ways, it shared as much value as an experience as a day mucking around at the river. The trip became part of our shared story. I am grateful for having been able to travel overseas, but I also know that adventure is a frame of mind and can cost nothing. Richness in our lives is found in our relationships with friends, family and community. Any experiences you share with others makes for a richer relationship, while binding you together forever in a distinctive and enduring way. It doesn't matter if money is spent to provide the experience.

CHANNELLING THE CREATIVE FORCE

Channelling the creative force and expressing yourself creatively is life-enhancing in every way possible. Whether you sing in the shower, make art, dance to the radio, play an instrument, sew, design, sculpt, build, garden or cook – whatever moves you to be creative will feed your soul. If you share this sense of creativity with your children, or they at least see and hear you being innovative, they will be influenced and perhaps inspired, and learn to value creative expression. Given the chance, your natural learners, in their own way, will start creating too, and inspiration may flow both ways. Allowing time to consciously create is good practice. It does not matter what the activity is, as long as there is some space to feel or express the imaginative and creative side of yourself.

For me personally, music can be transformative. It is a big part of my life. My days have soundtracks, music that promotes different moods to aid, match or change how I am feeling. Songs have carried deep meaning for me at different times in my life, inspiring me, urging me on, or providing comfort where needed. Do not underestimate the power of music. Young children soak up music that you play, and they also clock your response to it. Being able to create a mood, calm a situation, or express a feeling through music or other creative means can change your life. I have a bias towards music, but I know any creative endeavour contains a power all of its own.

MAGICAL MUSICAL MOMENTS
- Supporting an impromptu concert or show from kids
- Dancing with kids of all ages, sharing the fun of their music and moves
- Taking the time to teach a few ukulele chords when asked
- Playing guitar with the teenager whom you haven't seen all day who appears right on your bedtime (how can you refuse?)
- Making up your own songs, or new words to old songs, no matter how ridiculous they are, and sharing them with your children
- Dancing together and making up your own special moves for the next time you are at a dance or wedding, with your child as choreographer
- Sharing a song or a dance that is special

Giving yourself and your children permission to follow wherever your interests take you, and then feeling confident enough to express what emerges is a driving force in life. Being creative is a response to something deep inside us as humans, and it doesn't matter how it manifests. Being a parent of natural learners feels like the greatest expression of that creative spark, by first allowing you to tap into your creativity, and then them into theirs, as their individual spirits grow and are nurtured, and as they create their own truth each and every day.

THE LIFE-LONG GIFT OF NATURAL LEARNING

Gifting a life of natural learning to your kids is giving them a childhood of freedom. It may not always suit everyone for a multitude of reasons, but if you feel drawn to it and choose to pursue it, then be sure to give it your best. Breathe out, slow down and focus on sharing the joy your children offer. Nothing else could be more important. Giving the time and energy to your family will bring bountiful and unknown gifts to you all. The adventure of claiming your child's childhood for themselves and being there to share the fun is a journey of unknown depth and destination. You can write the script together and champion the odyssey as it unfolds.

Chapter 15

BEYOND THE IMAGINATION YEARS

My homeschooled children are now young adults who each love to analyse and reflect on their childhood and appreciate how great it was. As they look back and see it in its entirety they are grateful for the life we have had. The younger kids were 23, 21 and 18 when this book went to press. Included below are their perspectives and stories of how natural learning has worked out for them and where they are at now with their lives. But first, a word from my step-children Dane and Kim, who are now parents themselves. They may not be mentioned much in this book, but they have always been present.

None of the kids read the manuscript before writing their accounts, and they tell their story here in their own words.

DANE

I remember Jane joining our family of three when I was 11. For a number of years, it had been just Dad, my younger sister Kim and me, and we hadn't had a female role model to look up to. Jane was very warm to Kim and me and wanted to make sure that we were comfortable and that she wasn't coming into our lives to take Dad away from us.

In terms of parenting, Jane has been a massive influence on me. Right through my teenage years there were babies living with us. Hannah was born when I was 13 years old, and Charlie was born three weeks before I left for university as an 18-year-old.

I shared my teenage years with young children living in our bubble, but one big thing I remember during this time is that Jane was always there to talk to. Whether it was a passing comment or something more elaborate, she made time to listen. As a result, I was upfront and honest with her and I can remember telling her things (about relationships, girlfriends, friend trouble, etc) that I am pretty sure many teenage boys wouldn't share with their mum.

The second thing I remember is that Jane never said 'no'. Dad was in the hospitality industry during these formative years, working late nights and weekends, and so I guess I didn't see all that much of him during busy times. Most decisions and conversations, dealings, etc were through Jane, who ran the household and who by then was very much a part of my life and someone I considered to be my parent. I was always given permission to do what I wanted – visit friends, see my girlfriend, or head to a party on a Saturday night. I was always given full autonomy. Because of this I was open and honest with her, she knew the trust was mutual and there was an open dialogue that gave me the skills to deal with anything that came up.

I am now a parent of two boys under five. The influence of having Jane as my parent, and a natural parent at that, has been considerable. The language that I try to use with my children is positive, for instance, saying 'yes' and letting my boys experience as many things as possible, even if there is a risk of a bruise or scratch. The importance of relationships and forming connections is also important. But probably the biggest influence in this sphere is that of following interests and passions. As a parent and a current primary school teacher, I can see how incredibly engaged and motivated (and happy) children can be when they are doing what they want and when they want. What a cool way to learn, right?

I believe that learning happens in spades when we are having experiences and are exploring the world around us. We can help to create these opportunities for our children and give them time to do this, with our nurturing love and support – I think this is in essence what I have taken from Jane's parenting.

KIM

As a teenager in a house with a growing family I didn't pay much attention to the way Jane chose to parent. Instead I was preoccupied and possibly quite self-indulgent. Although I spent my first 10 years without Jane and went to school, her truth and dedication to raising my siblings has had a profound influence on the way I am parenting today.

It is definitely a subconscious effect and as I raise my babies I see now that I was partially paying attention to what I was witnessing. I have naturally practised attachment parenting, I co-sleep and I hope that as my children grow, I will continue to be influenced by Jane's parenting philosophies in some way.

My admiration for Jane as a mother and human is immense and I am so grateful that she has raised incredible, intelligent, independent and open-minded people that I get to call my siblings. As they say, the proof is in the pudding.

HANNAH

I find it really hard to talk about natural learning as a whole because education is a subjective experience, and so much of 'natural learning' is actually parenting. I think that it worked really well for me, but that doesn't mean that school wouldn't have – what worked well overall was how I was parented. Saying that, as I move further and further away from being a contrary teenager, the more I start to appreciate Mum's application of natural learning principles to our lives.

From the ages of eight to about 12, I think I mostly played and read books. I really agree with the idea that play, un-directed creativity and 'resourced' making is important for kids. I ended up making and doing a lot of things, from writing stories, to sewing, to making short films, to elaborate make-believe games with my friends. I was drawn towards stories, towards social, organisational games (made-up worlds with systems, newspapers, films, scripts, costumes, making food and planning 'cafes'). We went tramping, camping, to museums, to camps, to workshops, to concerts, to plays, to sleepovers, to music lessons and to shows. I remember it as an idyllic, carefree time. I really valued being able to spend that time freely, and definitely didn't miss out on things because I was at home.

My first few years were full of the kind of creativity that is really vital in childhood but has to undergo a transformation to something more structured in adolescence, or it disappears. This transformation, I think, makes creativity something that presents challenges – a social aspect to making things, a demand for practice, new ideas that show what you don't know. At around the age of 12, I stopped wanting to play make-believe. I didn't want to hang out with my family, and me and my friends had to find things to do – we couldn't just spend hours playing at being magical adventurers, or super versions of ourselves defeating evil in very cool outfits. This age coincided with my getting my own laptop for the first time, and so my time became filled with the internet. At first, a lot of it was very creative – our make-believe stories became little films, often horror movies that we watched during sleepovers. I dove into fan culture, which led to a run as a fanfiction author. I learned to use a photo editor to make edits and GIFs for my blog, and I spent hours editing our films. Four of us set up a film production 'company', and we took turns writing scripts, directing and producing. I really loved the organisational aspect of our little film sets – being the admin and assistant behind the scenes. I spent time playing music and hanging out with my friends, and a decent chunk of time online. Being 12 and 13 years old is not fun; for the first time you are unsure about a lot of things, like who you are in relation to other people, what you are meant to look like and what you do with your time, and the fact that the 'future' is a thing, and that your actions now will change what happens there. The internet was a mind-expanding escape from all those preteen existentialisms. By the age of 14 I'd pretty much stopped reading books altogether. I'd spent the whole summer watching multiple sci-fi TV shows from the 90s, and I was really starting to think about going to school just to get away from my (perfectly nice) family.

I ended up living in Switzerland for a year with some family friends and going to a Swiss high school. While I'd definitely learned some maths at home, as Mum said, it had been when I needed it for something, and I'd promptly forgotten it. Going into an equivalent NCEA L2 physics class was hilarious; even if I'd spoken German perfectly at the beginning, I wouldn't have understood anything. The other subjects were fine, and after six months I could participate a little in History, Literature and Art. I really enjoyed learning what I learned in Chemistry, although it really was only a little because I didn't have the vocabulary in German to learn as much as the others (I wasn't expected to keep up fully, as I was there to practise German). Socially, I definitely felt my age (I was about one year younger than most of my class, and the other exchange students were all 16-18 years old). However, this didn't make much of a difference after a few months, and I got enough of an understanding of what high school was to decide how I wanted to spend the next couple of years at home.

I came back immediately wanting to return to Europe. For this, I needed money, and so I needed a job. I found work cleaning, waitressing, and then at a lovely bookshop. At this point, I just wanted to get my university qualifications as quickly as possible, while making money, and therefore high school seemed like a waste of time. Doing the bare minimum, I could get my NCEA credits for uni in a year and a half online. I did level one Maths, level two English, and level three Classics, German, and History. I'd loved learning another language in Switzerland, and the structured, self-disciplined learning that it had entailed made me want to study more. While doing NCEAs via correspondence school I also attended Te Wananga o Aotearoa to study Te Reo Māori. This was another new learning environment, and one which I loved. I left home at 18 with my university entrance achieved, and a couple of plane tickets.

One of the big things that I'm noticing at this point in my life is the sense of agency that I was given through my childhood and adolescence. It's not just the idea that you can do whatever you want, but that if you want things to happen you have to make them happen – and you can make things happen. Sure, I could sit and read all day, or watch Buffy the Vampire Slayer for a whole summer, or glue stuff to my windowsill (sorry), but I also learned that if I wanted to make a film or a magazine with my friends, I had to organize it. If I wanted my NCEAs, or money, I had to study and I had to work. If I want to keep going to uni (and I do) I need to write my essay instead of watching YouTube. I'm not the most disciplined person in the world, but I really appreciate the sense of responsibility that I personally got from being unschooled. Like I said, natural learning is actually just parenting, so I guess that this is something that I appreciate about how I was parented. However, the specific ethos of the importance of play is something I really believe in, as is treating kids like the people that they are, and supporting them in their own creativity, drive and enthusiasm for life. I never felt like I needed to do any one thing, one accomplishment or strive for a particular job to make my parents happy or proud – happiness, kindness, and an appreciation for everything that we had and did were the focus.

The social aspect of not going to school is a big one for some people. Personally, we had a really social childhood and adolescence, not necessarily in the sense that we spent a lot of time with other people, but in the sense that our social relationships were important to us, and (I think) healthy. I'm quite an independent person, so I spent a decent amount of time doing things by myself, but when I wanted to hang out with people, I always did. My social circle broadened considerably when I was about 16, thanks to extracurricular activities like drama, politics, and music. I think that if homeschooling or unschooling becomes confined to just one family, or just the house, you might as well just go to school. A lot of what I learned, both socially and academically, actually happened away from home, especially when I was a teenager. We were surrounded by a community, both geographically and in terms of the natural learners group that we belonged to (and later, the wider networks that we found through extracurriculars). Although I'm still mentally kicking myself for spending two years mostly alone in my room on a computer when I was 13 and 14, I ended up spending the next two years being really social, in a range of situations.

At 21, I've come to realise that spending hours and hours on the internet each day isn't the healthiest way for me to live. I now understand that the less screen time I have, the better I feel, but I really sympathise with anyone trying to raise kids today. Screens are really prevalent, they're useful, they can be tools, and I certainly was formed both positively and negatively by the hours I spent on the internet. It became an often educational, often waste-of-time escape when I was a teenager. However, I'm really glad that I didn't get a computer or a phone before I was 12.

I'm in my third year of a Bachelor of Arts right now, majoring in Sociology and Te Reo Māori (with some English Literature thrown in there). University is very different from high school (and I don't hold it up as the gold standard of achievement for young people!). How you learned as a teenager becomes irrelevant, and what matters more are the life skills you picked up along the way, your relationships with other people, and how you treat people and your responsibilities. I love studying, but I'm so grateful that I was brought up to understand that life and your health and happiness always come first, and that learning happens along the way.

OLLIE

My experience as a natural learner

To be honest, I never really think of my upbringing as being that of a natural learner. It just feels like life, having just lived doing our own thing day to day. Some of the key moments I guess are the world trip, being a true pinnacle of my childhood. I think that was the transition from child to teenager. Getting to experience the world was a real eye opener at that age. I recently found Mum's blog (freedomanddreams.wordpress.com) and spent a few hours reading about our trip while wallowing in the joys and good memories that it stirred up. It is especially relevant with all my recent and current travels.

Our natural learning group was a key part too. All my time with Steve and the big boys at Forest School was very formative. Having that tribe and those role models at such a young age was amazing, plus all the other activities and opportunities such as the camps. These gave a pretty good community to be around, having that support and reassurance.

The creativity as well, the endless games. From shops to escaping across the Swiss mountains, making movies, building huts, army bases, medieval games and battles, surviving and tramping, sneaking and going on missions. All of these were inspired by something I/we had read or seen, or someone we had talked to. It was amazing to have the time, support and resources as well as love from Mum to be able to really immerse ourselves in these things which were really transformative and allowed great learning opportunities to unfold.

Having extended conversations and discussions about politics, world issues and everything else. Late night and dinner time debates were huge highlights.

Advantages of my upbringing are that I am able to think outside the box and step away from the mainstream and create my own life/ have my own perspective.

I have confidence in my worldly ability, having real skills and being able to build relationships with people from all walks of life.

I was able to explore my passions and what I wanted to do with my life, to learn about anything I want and what I think is useful.

I think I was fortunate to do things as a teenager that helped me develop my confidence and resilience. I believe it is critical while you are growing up to be challenged and pushed. In my case this came from martial arts, Cadets and Scouts as well as music, Duke of Edinburgh, and eventually school.

Mum found the perfect balance for me by finding people and opportunities for me to experience things such as competing, learning to accept loss and working with other people. I was able to gain a lot that I draw on now in life. I would say my life has had an ebb and flow, sort of up and down where I have had these highs that are amazing and then I start to fall. Every time I started to drop down Mum managed to come in and help me fly again. I think this is the role of a good parent. Not controlling their child but nudging them in the right direction. Not smothering them, but still being there to support when it is needed.

Here is what I mean:

Age 1–11 years. Amazing childhood, everything I could have asked for. I reach 11 years old and start to become a teenager and begin to lose direction and purpose. I was helped to find Taekwondo, which grew into my love for martial arts, one of the most transformative things I have ever done. Mum, especially, opened my eyes to other activities and opportunities.

Age 11–15 years. Everything is blooming. I excel at Scouts and Cadets as well as martial arts. These allow me to develop huge amounts of confidence, leadership skills, soft skills, teamwork and gain and build relationships. I take on board brass music and Duke of Edinburgh and life is perfect.

Age 15 years. While I have so much going on, I begin to lack purpose and direction again and Mum suggests school.

Age 16–18 years. School provides me with every opportunity I need. It gives me a huge social life, mental, physical and intellectual challenge and development.

Age 17–19 years. I go through some highs and lows as I become an adult. I am given a large amount of freedom and support to experiment and do what I want while always having a loving and open family and house to come back to. I see the paths that other people walk on, and after following them for a bit, I learn what is for me, and what is not for me. I learn what I am like at my best and at my worst. I am always able to talk and reflect on life with my family. Once again, I was nudged in the right direction while being allowed to make my own mistakes and learn and grow from them. Making mistakes and learning from them is probably the most important thing I did.

For my future there are many goals and ideas. To be honest, most of them absolutely scare me. Just thinking about them makes me realise I have a huge amount of self-doubt that I didn't always know was there. But then I realise I am 19 years old, living on the other side of the world. I have not seen my family or home country in months. I reflect on what I have done with my short life so far, and how I have stepped out of my comfort zone many times in the past, how I have faced self-doubt many times before. I feel as though my upbringing has given me such a great outlook on life. That life is more than a time to follow the norm, to wither away, paying bills then dying. Unschooling has opened my mind to the great wide world that exists, both the world outside and the even scarier and daunting world that exists within. I can summarise the things it has given me. A desire to live life to the full and the confidence to do that.

Unschooling my kids would depend on a number of factors, but ultimately it would depend on the child. What form of upbringing would give them the most opportunities?

CHARLIE

As of writing this, I've just turned 17. I'm driving my car on a restricted license, renting a studio to grow my video content creation business and trying to explore as much of the world as I can.

I don't feel like a kid anymore, but I also don't feel like I can fully look back on my childhood just yet.

That being said, there are a few things I have reflected on, but for the full analysis please pre-order my biography: 'The Rambler with the Camera'.

Anyway.

Freedom is what stands out in my mind. I had the freedom to play, explore, and above all else do my own thing. I have no doubt that it was the weeks I was allowed to convert our home into a diverse economy of shops, along with me being allowed to busk on the streets and earn real money at eight years of age, which created my interest in business.

Just like how I have no doubt that my parents not bothering me for 10 hours a day while I played with Lego contributed to my focus on and passion for storytelling.

Natural learning did the trick for me. I've always enjoyed self-educating, spending long periods of time on one project, having space and time to myself and choosing when to socialise, and with whom. So just as school seems to fit well for some of my friends, natural learning just seems to fit for me.

I value the confidence my childhood has left me with.

Perhaps not being tested and compared to other kids my age, on subjects I didn't enjoy, helped with this. Perhaps not feeling as much pressure to fit into social groups helped. Or maybe it helped being told it was worth chasing my passions and spending time on them.

As my brother, Mr Deputy Head Boy Oliver, so wisely said, 'Growing up just felt like living life.' We were operating in the 'real world,' often with a fair bit of independence and responsibility, and this would lead to me interacting with a lot of adults.

I must have observed how adults talked to each other (over the top of my Asterix book), and modelled my communication on that, rather than after the way you might talk to a teacher.

I suppose this gave me a base to hold a conversation and speak to those scary, tall, deep-voiced folk as if they were just a friend helping me build a Jedi Starfighter out of Lego. I started speaking to adults as equals at a young age, and this also must have helped my self-confidence.

Natural learning has given me the freedom to find my passions, the support to pursue them, and the independence to make them my own.

I think my biggest takeaway from it all is parenting. After all, that's what natural learning really is. It's the philosophy of how I've been raised which will stick with me, not the specifics of my education. Having freedom, playing, realising my passion, and taking my place in the world when I felt ready. That's what my childhood was, and I hope to give that to my children one day.

A WISH FOR THE JOYFUL LIFE

May your children inspire you to live with integrity and love.

May their wonder at the world be a reminder that you too are a life-long learner.

May you idle away hours watching scudding clouds, falling leaves and the setting sun.

May you spend hours reading aloud, cooking together, playing and dancing.

May the magic of nature's playground be where you and your child stop and rest for a while.

May your child be a catalyst for change in the world, simply by being themselves.

May you be brave enough to explore the potential of letting your child be who they were born to be.

May you be perfectly you and cease to strive to be a perfect parent.

May you use love as your guide, joy as a rudder, while you honour the captains of the ships you are sailing with on this wild and wonderful expedition.

FURTHER READING

freedomanddreams.wordpress.com, my blog

Holt, John, *How Children Learn,* Da Capo Lifelong Books, 1995, *How Children Fail,* Da Capo Lifelong Books, 1995, *Learning All the Time,* Da Capo Lifelong Books, 1990 www.johnholtgws.com

Montessori, Maria, *Citizen of the World,* The Montessori-Pierson Publishing Company, 2019 *Maria Montessori Speaks to Parents,* The Montessori-Pierson Publishing Company 2019, www.montessori.org.nz

Pikler, Emmi, thepiklercollection.weebly.com

Playcentre, www.playcentre.org.nz

Rosenberg, Marshall B, *Non Violent Communication,* PuddleDancer Press, 2003, nonviolentcommunication.com

Tracks and Tides Rites of Passage, www.tracks.net.nz

Weldon, Laura Grace, *Free Range Learning: How Homeschooling Changes Everything,* Hohm Press, 2010, lauragraceweldon.com

Jane Evans is a natural learning parent, teacher, writer and musician in Aotearoa New Zealand. With over 20 years of parenting and natural learning experiences and perspective, her advocacy for natural learning is as strong as ever. Having grown up children means there is now time for her to play more, following her own passions and to continue her own journey as a life-long learner.

Made in United States
North Haven, CT
06 May 2022